Transforming New Technologies into Cash Flow

Creating Market-Focused Strategic Paths for Business-to-Business Companies

Transforming New Technologies into Cash Flow
Creating Market-Focused Strategic Paths for Business-to-Business Companies

Roger More, PhD

Routledge
Taylor & Francis Group
NEW YORK AND LONDON

First published by
The Haworth Press, Inc., 10 Alice Street, Binghamton, NY 13904-1580

This edition published 2013 by Routledge

Routledge	Routledge
Taylor & Francis Group	Taylor & Francis Group
711 Third Avenue	2 Park Square, Milton Park
New York, NY 10017	Abingdon, Oxon OX14 4RN

PUBLISHER'S NOTE
The development, preparation, and publication of this work has been undertaken with great care. However, the Publisher, employees, editors, and agents of The Haworth Press are not responsible for any errors contained herein or for consequences that may ensue from use of materials or information contained in this work. The Haworth Press is committed to the dissemination of ideas and information according to the highest standards of intellectual freedom and the free exchange of ideas. Statements made and opinions expressed in this publication do not necessarily reflect the views of the Publisher, Directors, management, or staff of The Haworth Press, Inc., or an endorsement by them.

Cover design by Jennifer M. Gaska.

Library of Congress Cataloging-in-Publication Data

More, Roger, 1942-
    Transforming new technologies into cash flow : creating market-focused strategic paths for business-to-business companies / Roger More.
        p. cm.
    Includes bibliographical references and index.
    ISBN-13: 978-0-7890-3020-7 (hc. : alk. paper)
    ISBN-10: 0-7890-3020-9 (hc. : alk. paper)
    ISBN-13: 978-0-7890-3021-4 (pbk. : alk. paper)
    ISBN-10: 0-7890-3021-7 (pbk. : alk. paper)
    1. Technological innovations—Management. 2. Technological innovations—Economic aspects. 3. Marketing—Technological innovations. 4. Strategic planning. I. Title.

HD45.M667 2005
658.4'062—dc22
                                                                          2005019407

This book is dedicated to my daughter, Mary Kate,
who continues to delight me with her achievements,
and my wife, Nancy, who has supported me for so long.
They are the loves of my life.

ABOUT THE AUTHOR

Roger More, PhD, is a professor at the Ivey Business School at the University of Western Ontario in London, Canada. He previously served as a faculty member at Harvard Business School. Dr. More is principal of the management consultant firm of Roger More and Associates, specializing in the creation of focused strategic and marketing planning processes and leadership for technology-intensive companies. He formerly worked for Celanese Corporation as process engineer, project engineer, and assistant unit production superintendent.

Dr. More is lead co-author of *Winning Market Leadership* and has been widely published in respected journals, including the *Journal of Marketing, Journal of Product Innovation Management, Industrial Marketing Management, R and D Management, Journal of Business Research, IEEE Engineering Proceedings, Journal of the Operational Research Society,* and *Journal of Brand Management.* He is on the editorial boards of the *Journal of Business-to-Business Marketing* (The Haworth Press) and the *Journal of Product Innovation Management.*

CONTENTS

Preface

Many management books have been written on the strategic planning and development of new products. Others address the challenges of marketing new products. A whole literature has evolved around the management of technology. All of these books address in some way part of the most globally expensive and high-risk corporate management challenge of the future: the transformation of complex bundles of new physical technologies into highly profitable, cash-flow generating new products and competitive market strategies. In the real world of professional managers faced with these challenges, the strategic choices they have to make cannot be compartmentalized into the "neat boxes" of decisions presented in some of this extensive literature.

This book will identify managers who inhabit two different management worlds in companies: the world of physical technologies, and the world of buyers, customers, and competitive markets. Managers from these two worlds often see new technologies completely differently, and on a wide range of dimensions. In the midst of these differences, the managers must work together within companies to integrate technologies choices with other critical elements of market strategy, to try to manage the elusive market focus for their companies that drive cash flow.

This book is the result of working with such management teams for more than thirty years in many large, global, technology-intensive companies. This work has included a diverse range of complex technologies, product functionalities, market networks, and end-user market segments. The major objective of this book is to improve management teams' ability to integrate physical technology choices with the other critical strategic choices in market-focused strategies. A series of simple, powerful concepts and tools have been tested with managers to directly integrate four critical strategic bundles in specific competitive situations: technologies, product functionalities, market networks, and end-user segments. These strategic bundles are then directly linked to their capacity to generate net cash flow.

Managers who read and apply this book will find

- new concepts to break down and manage the four critical strategic bundles that connect technologies to market focus;
- simple and powerful tools to integrate the four primal choices with one another to create a market-focused strategy;
- recognition and management of six naturally occurring strategic transformation processes that knit the four primal strategic bundles to one another;
- the application of real, in-depth case examples to demonstrate the concepts and tools;
- tools to explicitly connect the primal strategic choices to the most valid objective for real financial success for new technologies and products, long-term net cash flow; and
- a Management Application Toolkit: simple worksheets management teams can apply to their real new technology and product opportunities.

Acknowledgments

The work represented in this book will always be a work in progress, evolving as I am privileged in my personal research and consulting to try to help more professional managers and companies with the "toughest game in town," transforming the explosion of complex and exciting new technologies facing them into bundled solutions that can be adopted by customers in highly competitive markets, and much more important, making real money for the companies involved. My greatest thanks to every one of the thousands of managers I have worked with for their roles in creating, shaping, and testing the ideas in this book.

Some of the companies that I have been privileged to work with include Celanese, General Electric, IBM, Atomic Energy of Canada (AECL), Textron, Noranda, DuPont, Nortel, Digital Equipment (DEC), Solvay, ICI, General Motors, Hewlett-Packard, The National Research Council, and Ciba-Geigy. There have been many others. In addition, thanks to the many managers I have worked with in executive education programs at Harvard Business School, Ivey Business School, Penn State, Duke Corporate Education, INSEAD, and IPADE.

Very special thanks is owed to longtime friend Joseph Greulich, former CEO of Solvay Plastics, for his intellectual contributions as we worked through many new technology and product challenges together. My greatest debt is to David Lichtenthal, editor of *Journal of Business-to-Business Marketing* and senior editor of The Foundation Book series in Business Marketing. He has been a supporter and friend, one of those rare individuals who takes risks, makes big promises, and delivers more. Without his help, the task of writing this book would have been much more difficult. Thanks to David Brown for our many useful and provocative discussions regarding new technology over the years, and for his support.

The Haworth Press managers and team have impressed me at every turn with their competence, professionalism, warm manner, and accessibility. Special thanks to Peg Marr and Tara Davis. Great thanks is also due my gifted associate Jodi Guthrie for her painstaking and excellent work with me in crafting and improving the many drafts of the manuscript.

Last, profound thanks to my colleagues at the Ivey Business School for their support, in particular, Don Barclay, Terry Deutscher, Adrian Ryans, Craig Dunbar, and other members of the marketing area group.

Chapter 1

Overview of the Book

The distinguishing characteristic of great professional managers is their capacity to constantly reconceptualize the bases for competitive strategy by creating, recognizing, and applying powerful new concepts to their reality. This book is for them.

Roger More (2005)

In the future, most business-to-business companies will see the greatest explosion of incredible and complex new technologies ever imagined, on both the supply and competitive market sides of companies and the market networks surrounding them. Most of these new technologies will have to be bundled with many others in order to create competitively differentiated product functionality for end users. In the face of this explosion, the majority of these new technologies will not make money for companies investing heavily in developing, adopting, and bundling them. In every industry, there will be some huge losers. Many technologies that succeed in the lab will fail in the competitive marketplace. Many companies will lose significant amounts of net cash flow. All of these phenomena are already clearly visible in today's competitive market realities.

This book argues that the primary causes of these failures are the companies' lack of market focus, their flawed and incomplete concepts for what market focus means, and their critical interactions with technology choices. In many companies, technology choices are completely and explicitly divorced from competitive market strategy. Many managers have huge conceptual gaps in the processes they go through when making choices and explicitly integrating the four critical and extremely complex strategic choice bundles: technologies, product functionalities, market networks, and end-user customer segments. In many companies, managers have a difficult time integrating technology choices with these other critical areas of choice in marketing strategies. Numerous examples of these failures will be cited.

The major corporate challenge addressed by this book is helping managers in their complex processes of understanding, planning, creating, and sustaining market focus for new technologies, transforming these into rapidly adopted new products, and integrating these technologies into focused choices for other strategic bundles critical to their success. In too many companies, the choices, focus, development, adoption, and bundling of new technologies are completely removed from the strategic and marketing choices that are profoundly driven, influenced, and constrained by them. This book will reconceptualize market focus as a strategic-path focus in a managerially powerful way.

In many companies, the development, adoption, and bundling of new and exciting technologies are funded and transformed into new products based on their own physical and technological merits by different managers than those who plan the competitive market strategy, in isolated organizational processes, and without concern for or analysis of their impact on other critical choices, such as product functionalities, end-user segment needs, market networks fit, competitive differentiation, or the capacity to create net cash flow. As a result, many "technology breakthroughs" become "cash flow catastrophes." As Fusfeld pointed out, "despite the obvious role of technology in superlatively successful enterprises, technological issues only occasionally are included explicitly in typical corporate strategy reviews, and only rarely are they among the regular inputs to corporate planning and development."[1]

This book reflects not only the development and testing of new concepts for managers, but also thirty years of rich personal experience working with managers in companies competing in technology-intensive business-to-business markets, who are faced with a wide spectrum of exciting new technology and product cases. My role as a consultant and leader of executive workshops has been to help teams of managers, faced with complex new technology and product opportunities, to improve their strategic choice processes, to create and sustain the critical but elusive market focus, and to generate high levels of net cash flow.

In the harsh competitive realities faced by these professional managers, market focus means consistently creating and sustaining focused choices of specific new technologies and products, and supporting market strategies to generate high long-term net cash flow. In working with these managers, it has been evident that this is one of the most difficult set of strategic choices they face on a continuing basis. An immediate reflection of this struggle with market focus is the high and growing failure rate for new technologies and products.

Many diverse and complex new technology and product case examples will be cited in this book, including car navigation systems, semiconductors, fuel cells, medical imaging, and synthetic blood. It is critical that several different case examples be explored in specific detail, so that the generic power of strategic paths can be clearly illustrated in real situations. Two very different major case examples featured are fuel cells and synthetic blood. However, the concepts illustrated in these case examples are entirely generic and applicable to any set of technologies, product functionalities, market networks, and end-user buyer segments.

Both fuel cells and synthetic blood have had a mixed history of success and failure for many applications and companies involved, each pursuing a complex variety of different strategic paths. A recent article noted that "fuel cells were to revolutionize the way autos are powered," but "bringing the technology to market has proved difficult."[2] At the center of the challenge is the choice of strategic paths. The authors note that "finding a fuel cell with the right combination of features has proved difficult. That's because it must be lightweight and compact enough to fit under the hood of a car, yet still capable of delivering power, acceleration and durability at a cost that drivers expect."[3] The authors clearly recognize the problems of integrating technologies, product functionalities, and other sets of critical strategic choices and bundles.

In financial success terms, the management problem of developing new technologies and transforming them into high-net-cash-flow new products is by far the most important and high-risk corporate competitive problem. The total corporate investments globally in new technologies in the future will dwarf the investments in any other strategic decision area. One of the major impacts of this management reality is the new technology-development/adoption gap.

For most technology-intensive companies, the rate of development of new technologies is vastly greater than their end-user customer market's and market network's ability to adopt these new technologies in the form of new products. This gap is growing exponentially year by year, and points out the desperate need for increased market focus. In the previous fuel cell example, the authors note that cash flow is an issue. Making reference to Ballard Power Systems, a leading company in the fuel cell industry, the authors note "some analysts fear Ballard may run out of cash before it can start commercial production."[4] This difficult reality will be further explored in this book in the discussion of strategic paths, the cash flow dynamic, and the financial objectives for new technologies and products.

Looking at the total financial commitment and risk involved for fuel cells, the authors note that "at least fifty companies in North America, Europe, and Japan are developing fuel cells and related systems and components for the auto industry." They also note that "together, companies are spending in excess of $2 billion (U.S.) annually on fuel cell technologies. When government grants are added on the amount of spending likely tops $4 billion."[5] Clearly, the choices of technologies and related strategic choices represent huge levels of investment and risk. Equally, justifying a $4 billion total investment means that some companies competing in these markets will eventually have to generate net cash flows in the high billions to make any real net cash flow gain, and fairly soon, given the discounted cash flows. How likely is this to happen? These conditions are all too typical for new technology-driven markets.

Creating and sustaining market focus demands that corporate managers and teams must continuously make clear and early choices (yes and no) of which new technologies and product bundles to commit resources to and develop. The number of *no* choices is already becoming dramatically greater than the number of *yes* choices for highly market-focused companies. In the future, managers are going to have to be much better and stronger at making clear and early choices of new products and technologies on which to focus. This is a continuing challenge for many companies. Indeed, the recent problems of Hewlett-Packard in their acquisition of Compaq computers could be characterized as a huge loss of market focus, with a short-term explosion of technologies, end-user segments, product functionalities, and market networks for managers of the combined companies to attempt to manage. Given this explosion of strategic paths, it is likely that a significant number of them were losing cash flow.

In making these strategic choices for new technologies and products, managers are surrounded by complex and difficult corporate organizational realities, strategic choices, and existing corporate, strategic, and market-planning processes. A desperate need exists for simple and powerful new concepts to improve market focus and to simplify the processes managers go through in making these important strategic choices. It is critical that new concepts fit with and build on current realities and organizational processes managers face when they explore specific real, new technology and product opportunities.

Strategic paths represent a new and tested concept to help managers and teams in their decision processes to define, map, clarify, and quickly explore different integrated bundles of focused strategic choices for new technologies and products throughout their life cycle. It is a process to explicitly link physical technology choices with their impact on other critical strategic choices. In reconceptualizing market focus, four primal and critical strategic bundles have been developed. These four complex strategic bundles drive and constrain all of the other major strategic choices managers have to make for new technologies and products. Each of the four strategic bundles represents a complex set of choices that are independently very difficult to make. Combining these choices in a coherent strategy, making all four sets of choices in a way that is integrated, focused, and that creates strategic synergies, represents a major challenge for managers.

A MANAGEMENT PROCESS PERSPECTIVE

This book is predicated and based on a management process perspective, which is a cultural, research, and pedagogical hallmark of both Harvard and Ivey Business Schools. In principle, it means that in the realities facing professional managers, the success or failure of new technologies and products within a particular company culture and competitive situation is the result of the complex and interwoven human and organizational decision processes that managers and teams go through over time, and a result of the myriad competitive factors that influence success, many of which are completely out of managers' control. Ultimately, success or failure is the result of strategic choices managers make regarding analysis, planning forms, tools, methodologies, calculations, and optimizing solutions, among others. Tools and concepts, as with training drills for athletes, are designed to help managers ask the right questions in their strategic choice processes, not to do it for them.

Accordingly, the concept of strategic paths outlined in this book is intended to help managers raise and address a new set of critical strategic questions during their technology, market, and strategic-planning processes—not to replace their entire process of choosing and bundling new technologies and products. It is a new and additional tool that can strengthen and clarify critical areas of analysis and decision making in corporate market and strategic planning. The strategic paths presented in this text can help managers in different functional areas integrate their strategic decisions more effectively.

Management Process As a Team-Questioning Process

A critical part of the management process perspective is how managers conceptualize their strategic and market planning processes. Too often planning processes are conceptualized as the documentation of the process, or the written "plan." Some major problems with managers seeing written plans as processes are the following:

- The half-life of technology-intensive, competitive strategies today and in the future is rapidly diminishing. As a result, many new technology and product documented plans may be obsolete two weeks after they are written.
- Continuous iteration in the planning process is vitally important. When written plans and estimates are too extensively documented it makes it difficult for managers to quickly revisit and revise them.
- Frequently, in companies with these extensively documented plans, of necessity, many different functional managers and teams write their section of the plan in isolation, as though their strategic choices stand alone. Any hope of real strategic integration and focus is lost.
- The same applies to major changes in strategy, which are inevitable. If these are partitioned in the written plan, then so will be the revisions.

All of the previously mentioned problems are due to companies and managers misconceptualizing what great market-focused planning has to be as a process, and how the companies and managers drive market strategy in reality. A management process perspective is shown in simple form in Figure 1.1. In exploring this perspective, several key parts of the management process are involved. In looking at how market focused different companies are, each of these process factors and their effective management play a central role.

Management Teams

Management teams, informal or formal, are at the center of management process and potential market-focused strategies. Clearly, the process in which the teams are organized, and the way they conceptualize, articulate, analyze, and make strategic choices regarding competitive opportunities will have a huge impact on market focus. As a result, this book explores the critical conditions for effective teams in Chapter 7. This book stresses the potential power of highly focused management teams exploring different strategic paths for potential market focus.

The Central Role of Questions in Management Process

In all its different situations, planning in any context involves people asking series of questions and responding with choices, usually after doing some analysis. As shown in Figure 1.1, in reality, management teams plan at every level by asking specific strategic questions,

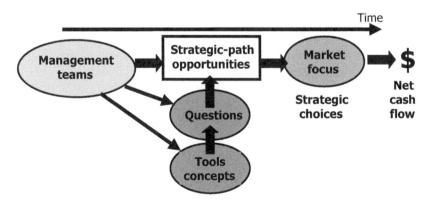

FIGURE 1.1. Team-questioning management process perspective.

then responding to these questions with strategic choices backed by the most powerful analyses they can apply. As a result, strategic plans, and the planning documents that accompany them, are only as powerful as the questions asked and the analysis and strategic choices that follow. An excellent example of a set of critical strategic market planning questions for general competitive situations can be found in a recent textbook, *Winning Market Leadership.*[6]

THE ROLE OF TOOLS AND CONCEPTS IN MANAGEMENT PROCESS

As shown in Figure 1.1, tools and concepts play an important role in management process. Applied badly, in some companies managers expect tools and concepts to actually make the strategic choices for them (for example, internal rate of return financial calculations, market attractiveness matrices, etc.). In fact, the only real utility of tools and concepts is to help managers frame the most critical strategic questions in their pursuit of market focus. This is exemplified by the concept of strategic-path analysis. The analysis's power is to bolster the capacity of management teams to clearly define and conceptualize complex strategic bundles and their individual and interactive strategic impact on market focus.

APPLYING MANAGEMENT PROCESSES

At the center of the management process perspective is how new concepts and processes are applied by managers to help them make better strategic choices. Four critical stages are involved: process decomposition, process mapping, strategic analysis, and strategic integration. Each stage plays a vital role in the exploration of strategic paths.

Process Decomposition

All of the factors and major choices in complex strategies for new technologies and products cannot be explored at once. The major factors in the process must be decomposed. For example, strategic paths allow managers and teams to break down the major strategic choices into four primal sets so that they can focus on one set at a time. Within each major set of strategic choices a further breakdown exists, so that each area can be subjected to in-depth scrutiny.

Process Mapping

Once the critical strategic choices have been decomposed, managers need to map the critical choices and organize them for analysis. In mapping strategic paths, for example, potential technology choices are mapped against product functionality choices to try to identify synergistic combinations. In mapping different strategic combinations, the most powerful approach is to map strategic dyads: two sets of choices and their complex interaction with each other. In doing the analysis, managers find working in two dimensions much easier and more focused.

Strategic Analysis

In exploring different maps of strategic combinations, managers and teams can quickly look at a wide range of strategic paths for analysis. This analysis is outlined in exhaustive detail in Chapter 8, in which a Management Application Toolkit provides detailed worksheets to help managers and teams carry out the analysis of strategic paths.

Strategic Integration

At some point in the iterative process of strategic-path exploration, managers must pull the different maps and analyses together into an integrated strategic path. This is the most challenging part of the strategic-path process.

THE CONCEPT OF STRATEGIC PATHS: STRATEGIC BUNDLES

For a particular competitive market opportunity, a strategic path is made up of four critical strategic choice bundles:

- Choice of technologies bundle
- Choice of product functionalities bundle

- Choice of market networks bundle
- Choice of end-user customer segments bundle

The strategic centrality, importance, and relationships of these complex bundles will be outlined in detail. For competitive opportunities of any technological complexity, these bundles can represent hundreds if not thousands of strategic choices, with interactions in many cases approaching the infinite. For any particular competitive opportunity, conceptualizing, defining, and developing the bundle of choices in each area and creating an integrated bundle with the greatest strategic focus, competitive differentiation, and synergy is the objective of the strategic-paths concept. It represents an incredibly difficult management challenge.

It is critical to understand what integration of these strategic bundles means. It is not just a matter of managers organizing the bundles that is always necessary, it is the process of teams of managers simultaneously, continuously, and iteratively planning and managing the integration to come up with highly competitively differentiated strategic paths.

DEVELOPING THE STRATEGIC-PATHS CONCEPT: A GROUNDED MANAGEMENT RESEARCH PROCESS

Consistent with the previously outlined management process perspective, the concepts developed in this book were evolved over time in an informal, evolutionary, and flexible real-time research approach grounded in deep and extensive relationships with senior managers facing real new technology and product cases rather than the traditional, academic, historical, data-based empirical approach. This grounded research process is shown in Figure 1.2 as a series of loose, iterative phases over time.

Management Relationships

The grounded management research process began and was sustained by management relationships. For the purposes of this book, this meant the series of relationships with managers in a large number of global technology-intensive companies in the context of project consulting and management workshops over a period of many years.

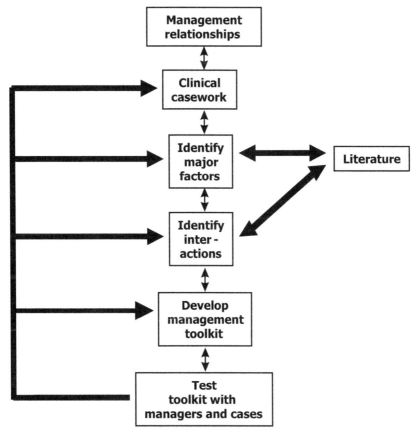

FIGURE 1.2. The grounded research process.

The nature of this work involved specifically defined new product case situations actually facing managers in the companies involved and the teams of managers responsible for developing and managing these new products and technologies. The new technologies and products themselves covered a wide range of industries and companies over a significant period of time. The most important aspect of these relationships is that they involved real and diverse managers, new technologies, new products, and competitive situations. Managers involved in this research process were making decisions to go forward into real marketplaces with competitive strategies. The risks and payoffs involved were significant and real.

The clear objective of this research was not to empirically develop or test a theory, but rather to develop powerful process tools that help managers.

Clinical Casework

In the process of developing the strategic-path concept, the clinical casework involved teams of managers trying to determine whether specific new products and technology case situations were worthy of investing in, and the strategies that might make the products successful. A large variety of worksheets were developed, tried, and applied in working with managers to try to develop improved choice processes.

In this clinical casework the approach was quite different from the traditional academic approach in which variables are defined in advance by a theory, measured homogeneously in every case, then analyzed mathematically to deduce causality. The casework on which this book is based was evolutionary and flexible. As we worked with managers over time on different cases, different questions were asked, different processes and worksheets were used, and a constant effort was made to identify the major generic questions that managers needed to analyze and pursue.

The focus in this research was on the questions managers needed to ask when looking at the potential success and failure of different strategic paths, not on precisely measuring homogeneous characteristics of the cases and connecting them to success and failure. The objective was to develop a process based on major questions that needed to be identified, asked, and acted upon in pursuit of successful technologies and products. Each clinical case was very different. They cut across many different industries, technologies, products, market networks, and end users.

IDENTIFYING MAJOR GENERIC STRATEGIC CHOICES AND QUESTIONS

The search for the major factors to drive the major questions in looking at new technologies and products was an evolutionary and flexible search. However, it became evident early on that the four major situational factors, or bundles, were of enormous central importance. Choice of technologies, end-user segments, product functionalities, and market networks clearly were the dominant decisions to be made in case after case that managers had to consider.

Moreover, in discussions with managers and work on cases with them it became clear that most of the other major strategic choices were driven by the previously mentioned four. Having identified these four, the work on the clinical casework continued, and the use of these four major factors was tested over and over again with various sets of worksheets to hone and refine the nature of the questions.

The ongoing measure of relevance and importance of these factors was the reaction of the managers when going through the worksheets and when trying to come to choices with respect to the specific technologies and products involved. It was their perception of how useful this material was for them that was the guiding feature of all of this research.

THE MANAGEMENT LITERATURE

The management literature was thoroughly explored for corroboration and support for the four major strategic choices that define strategic paths. For example, Gaynor notes the critical centrality of technologies, products, and market dimensions (including market networks) in new products planning.[7] He reports huge reductions in new product design and cycle times when these critical strategic choices are planned and managed together. He notes

> that may appear obvious, but most organizations continue to treat technology and markets independently rather than as a unit. Products rely on technologies; products depend on markets. New technologies without product or market applications provide no benefit. New products without new technologies provide a minimum benefit. Products without markets, regardless of their internally perceived benefits, consume resources without benefit.[8]

Similarly, Roberts and Meyer identify the following four strategic questions as the primal choices to be made regarding new technologies and product strategy.[9] In their words, "new product decision making in the technology-based enterprise addresses four basic issues":

- What are the basic needs or user functions that the firm will satisfy with its products?
- What are the groups of customers that share these needs or functional requirements and to whom the product will be sold?
- What technology will be used to build the products, and what is the source of that technology?
- What distribution mechanisms will be employed to bring successfully developed products to the marketplace?[10]

Burgelman, Maidique, and Wheelwright identify a very similar set of primal strategic choices:

- the deployment of technology in the firm's product-market strategy to position itself in terms of differentiation (perceived value or quality) and delivered cost, and to gain technology-based competitive advantage
- the use of technology, more broadly, in the various activities comprised by the firm's value chain
- the firm's resource commitment to various areas of technology
- the firm's use of organizational design and management techniques to manage the technology function[11]

In the authors' words, "these constitute four substantive dimensions of technology strategy."[12] Numerous other literature sources substantiate the previously identified four primal strategic choices in new technology and product situations.

IDENTIFYING STRATEGIC INTERACTIONS: TRANSFORMATION PROCESSES

One of the most interesting questions that came up in the course of working with managers and developing strategic-path concepts was the nature of the strategic interactions between the four major choices on a strategic path. It became evident in working through case situations that the interactions between the four strategic choices were critically important, and that a major problem in strategy was managing, reconciling, and integrating these four major bundles of decisions. When it was recognized that six major interactions occurred between the four major decision bundles, it became evident that it could be powerful to focus on these interactions.

These six strategic interactions have been characterized in this book as transformation processes. Each of the six is a complex management process that must be explicitly planned and mapped in order to manage their interactions.

CONCEPTUALIZING SUCCESS FOR NEW TECHNOLOGIES AND PRODUCTS

For this book, the ultimate measure of the success of technologies, products, and strategic paths will be clearly conceptualized as long-run positive net cash flow over a relevant time horizon. The validity of this measure in planning and managing strategic focus for new technologies and products will be outlined and developed.

Helping managers translate strategic paths into high long-term positive net cash flow is a critical objective of this book. As will be outlined, one of the major problems in managing strategic focus for new technologies in many companies is the huge and confused range concepts of success and their measures for new technologies and products found in corporate and management practice. These different success concepts and measures represent a confusing and often conflicting set of criteria, and are a major cause of the difficulty managers and companies encounter when creating successful new products and technologies.

The Concept of Transformation Processes

In focusing and integrating the four major strategic bundles on a strategic path, six complex transformation processes are identified and are critical to manage. The following list is the natural set of six strategic interactions between any four strategic bundles. These transformation processes are the following:

- The technologies→product functionalities transformation process
- The technologies→market networks transformation process
- The technologies→end-user segments transformation process
- The product functionalities→market networks transformation process
- The product functionalities→end-user segments transformation process
- The market networks→end-user segments transformation process

Management of these six transformation processes means that the strategic bundles in each critical area have to be purposefully planned, managed, mapped, and integrated with the other bundles in order to create mutual strategic focus, competitive differentiation, and strategic synergies. This is obviously not an easy task. As with managing any complex process, the strategic-path concept is used to decompose these six transformation processes into a series of powerful maps for careful exploration and analysis.

The Concept of Strategic Hot Zones

In this book, the creation of strategic hot zones is developed. A strategic *hot zone* is created by explicitly mapping and managing the six transformation processes so that focus and differentiation in one of the four critical strategic bundles creates and supports focus and differentiation in other bundles. Clearly, this is a difficult task. Hot zones may not always be possible. In this book, the example of fuel cells is extensively used to illustrate this concept along with a number of others.

Managing Strategic Paths: Creating Multifunctional and Transformation Project Teams

Chapter 7 of this book outlines the corporate imperative to have explicit organizational mechanisms in place for managers and teams to conceptualize, plan, and manage strategic paths. This is a difficult challenge. A new concept of *transformation teams* has been developed to map project team members onto strategic paths to improve team focus and process. These transformation teams make members of multifunctional project teams explicitly responsible for different transformation processes.

DEVELOPMENT OF THE MANAGEMENT APPLICATION TOOLKIT

During this long conceptual research and development process, a detailed management toolkit was evolved and tested to allow managers to easily ask the questions developed in this process in an organized, thoughtful, and iterative way. The toolkit in this book presents a series of mapping processes as worksheets, and these have been tested on many cases.

THE MANAGEMENT APPLICATION TOOLKIT

It is important to note that this book is focused on concepts and tools for managers and is set up so that these managers can apply the tools to specific new technology and product opportunities. The final chapter of this book is a Management Application Toolkit, which presents a set of simple and tested maps and worksheets that managers and teams can apply to specific new technology and product choices to quickly explore and test existing and new strategic path possibilities. The Toolkit encourages and rewards simple, creative, iterative, and rapid management team strategic mapping and experimentation, which is very powerful in the rapidly changing world of new technologies. It includes interactive cash flow spreadsheets that are simple and fast to use, and encourage the rapid estimation of the cash flow impacts of changes in strategic paths.

Consistent with the book, the Toolkit is not intended to be an exhaustive new technology and product planning process, but rather a powerful additional tool for managers to apply.

USING THE BOOK

This book is intended for professional managers, both present and future. It has been applied by many managers in companies facing exciting new competitive technology and product opportunities. It can also be used in teaching situations with MBA and executive MBA students in business school courses involving new technologies, new products, marketing planning, and strategic planning. It's most powerful application is in specific competitive new technology and product situations.

Chapter 2

Strategic Paths:
Reconceptualizing Market Focus

INTRODUCTION

What is market focus? What is market-focused strategy? Simply put, it is a company's management capacity to continuously and clearly focus and refocus strategic resources on the portfolio of competitive market opportunities at every level of the company that creates maximum long-term net cash flow. Companies with high and sustained market-focused strategies are highly conscious of the competitive and net cash flow characteristics of their entire evolving portfolio, all the way down to the lowest possible competitive strategic level of their organization.

It is important to note that the term *market focus* is seen in many different contexts in different companies. In practice, it can mean many different things in different company situations and cultures. The concept of market focus as outlined in this book is not often seen. The reasons for this will be made clear.

In this context, for most technology-intensive companies competing in business-to-business competitive markets, by far the greatest future strategic investments, costs, and risks will be in the development, adoption, bundling, and transformation of new technologies into competitive new products. The global rate of development of new technologies in every significant area is accelerating exponentially. As this is happening, it is clear that the individual and collective global capacity of end-user customers and market networks to adopt the exploding product applications of these technologies is not growing nearly as fast. This has led to a significant, long-term, and exponentially growing gap between the rate of development of technologies and the capacity of end customers and market networks to absorb them in the form of new products.

This development-adoption gap can have a dangerous temporal component: an initial surge of applications and rapid adoption for a dramatic new technology, filling the initial early adopter-segment demand, followed by a huge drop-off in adoption rate as slower adoption occurs for different end-user customer segments and short-term market saturation. The modern example of the telecommunications and wireless technology markets and the dramatic slowdown of Nortel, its suppliers, and other companies, is evidence that this gap is real and likely to become much more serious in the future.

A major implication of this development-adoption gap for technology-intensive companies is clear: Managers have to make faster, tougher, earlier, and clearer choices of market focus, choosing on which technologies, product functionalities, end-user market segments, and market networks to focus competitive market strategies and, more important, on which not to. Timing of market entry, growth, stasis, decline, and exit have become much more critical. These market focus choices will force managers to say no far more often than yes to new technology and product opportunities. Moreover, managers will have to make more exit choices for situations that initially looked attractive, then changed.

The problem can be even more serious. Even given a high-potential and exciting technology, the choice of which market end-user segments to serve, which product functionalities to develop, and which market networks to use to deliver the strategy represents a huge and growing range of alternative possibilities. It is all too easy to make poor choices.

This book will outline and develop a new concept of strategic-path creation and management that can help managers and teams to make better, clearer, and faster choices of strategic focus for their new technologies and products.

Strategic Paths: The Concept of Strategic Bundles

Strategic paths represent the four primal and most critical competitive spaces. They also represent the strategic choice bundles that define strategic focus and drive net cash flow for new technologies and products. These four critical strategic-path choices are listed here:

- Choice of technologies bundle
- Choice of product functionalities bundle
- Choice of end-user market segments bundle
- Choice of market networks bundle

These four overarching strategic choice bundles drive and constrain all other major strategic choices that managers and teams must make as the new technology and products are developed and introduced to markets. The entire market and competitive strategy flows from the four bundles, and is driven or constrained by them. These four generic and critical bundles must be mutually focused and strategically integrated in order for a new technology and the resulting product functionality to have a chance of producing high net cash flow. For many companies, this is often not the case.

MANAGERS' REALITIES: NEW TECHNOLOGIES AND PRODUCTS

The competitive realities facing managers in technology-intensive companies are frequently very different from those depicted in many theories, and are in fact much more difficult. Teams of managers looking at new technologies and products are faced with a significant number of extremely difficult choices surrounded by many variables that will affect the outcome, many of which are out of their control.

Some of the challenging characteristics of new technology and product opportunities facing managers are explained in the following sections. Each represents a major set of competitive challenges. Together, they can seem overpowering.

Individual Technology Choices

Most products of any complexity have more than ten, and in some cases hundreds, of individual technologies. In the case of highly technological products, such as wireless computing products or aircraft engines, the number of choices available regarding each individual component is very high, even though some of the choices may be standardized. These individual technology choices don't just apply to the product itself, but to all of the upstream and downstream manufacturing processes involved, to the companies' manufacturing processes themselves, and to a whole host of adopted and enabling technologies that may surround the product.

Laptop computers are an easy example. Despite their seemingly similar appearance, the number of different individual technology components available to erect their functionality is huge and growing very rapidly. Even choosing the individual technologies is a major challenge for competing companies.

Potential Technologies Bundles

In addition to all of the individual technology choices represented, the technologies must be bundled into products. These technology bundles usually comprise some existing technologies, some old technologies, and some new. In addition, some of the technologies may be exotic, and others may be simple and well known. Some may be developed, others adopted. Some may be product technologies, others manufacturing process technologies. Some may be hardware, some software.

When you look at the number of individual technology choices involved, these bundles can literally have an infinite number of permutations and combinations of technologies for a particular new product. In the case of laptops, each is a complex bundle of hundreds of individual technology choices. Many laptops may look similar in their functionality, but may have very different technology bundles.

Potential Product Functionalities Bundles

Product functionalities are clearly distinguished from product technologies in this book. Product functionalities represent the complex sets of perceptions by customers of the differentiated and useful comparative performance attributes of a product. Just as a huge array of technology bundles exists with many new products, a similarly huge number of potential product functionalities bundles exists: a large number of product attributes that can create utility and differentiation for end-use customers. These product functionalities are directly linked to the choice of technologies and vice versa.

Clearly, the bundles of technologies must be strategically integrated with the bundles of product functionalities since one produces the other. This presents a major challenge to managers in technology-intensive firms in terms of how to bundle and position the functionalities. Again, laptops are an excellent example. Large differences in product functionalities exist between many different laptops. Linking these to the best technology bundles is a big challenge.

Potential End-User Market Segment Bundles

Just as a large number of technology choices, bundled technology choices, and product functionality bundled choices exist, a growing number of end-user market segment bundles are coming into existence. Many markets for technology-intensive products have become more and more fragmented globally, with more and more precise user demands and differentiation created across a wider range of segments. This necessitates a much more difficult and focused set of choices to be made by new product and technology developers regarding which end-user market segments they will target.

For laptops, the number of distinctly different end-user segments is huge, ranging from high school students to nuclear scientists, and from individuals to large corporations. Each segment has very different product functionality needs as well as many other strategic and competitive characteristics.

Potential Market Network Bundles

In addition to the large number of end-user market segments, recent years have seen an explosion in the number of market networks that can access different segments. We have seen the addition of the Internet, open and closed intranets, and virtual networks combined with physical and logistical supply chains, value chains, and distribution networks. These networks encompass a growing array of delivering product functionality to end-user segments, as well as logistics, information flows, and many other roles. Many end-user segments are touched by a large number of market networks. This represents another difficult choice for managers faced with these new technology and product situations.

Regarding laptops, an explosion in the number and complexity of the market networks involved in their manufacture, distribution, service, and application has occurred, including the Internet and all its complexity.

THE MANAGERS' DILEMMA:
TWO DIFFERENT MANAGEMENT WORLDS

An important and complex underlying reason for many of the difficulties managers encounter when trying to successfully transform new technologies into high net cash flow strategic paths lies in the natural existence of two dramatically different management worlds within and between companies: the world inhabited by "technology" managers, and the world inhabited by "marketing, sales, and business" managers. These often disparate worlds, with different cultures, mind-sets, education, reward systems, time horizons, expectations, corporate roles, perspectives on the purpose of new technologies, and a host of other differences are shown in simple form in Figure 2.1. This does not mean that some managers cannot manage well in both worlds; indeed, many breakthrough technologies and new products have come from renaissance managers who created the physical technologies as well as their transformation into incredible and profitable new product functionality. But these people are rare in companies, both in terms of their personal characteristics and their functional roles and power.

These two worlds were recognized by Burgelman and Sayles.[1] They noted the great differences between the managers who inhabit either the physical technology world or the new product functionality world in terms of their work environment, professional orientation,

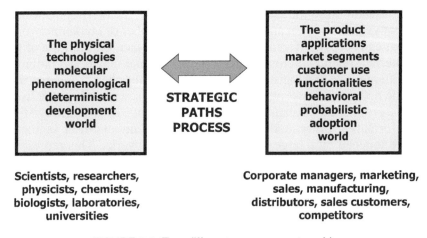

FIGURE 2.1. Two different management worlds.

education, and personal interests. These differences can make it difficult for managers from separate worlds to communicate or work together. Worse, they may conceptualize strategic paths very differently, and in conflicting ways.

The Physical Technologies World

One management world that exists in many technology-intensive companies and the competitive markets that surround them is the physical technologies world. As shown, it is the deterministic world of real, tangible, and often very complex physical and molecular process and product technologies and their evolution over time. This world involves scientists, researchers, engineers, technicians, and other people inside companies and research facilities who work in the physical realm. It is an entirely physical, phenomenological world. It is often a very internalized world. Managers in this world can create and develop highly differentiated, unique, and exciting technologies and bundles. This world includes product, process, systems, and manufacturing technologies, both on the supply side and the market side.

A good example of this world is the technologies bundle in laptop computers, which are complex bundles of literally hundreds of individual technologies. Managers in this world develop semiconductor chips, boards, wiring, transducers, transformers, connectors, bus bars, circuits, hardware, and software using extremely complex process, lab, and manufacturing equipment and systems. Many of these developers are narrow, technical specialists who have a unique understanding of their own technologies and cannot easily explain them to anyone else in the company. Imagine a nontechnical sales manager in a semiconductor fabrication plant listening to an engineer explain the details of how to etch a silicon wafer!

Unfortunately, these technologies, by themselves, can be potentially strategically useless to the other world. They become useful only when they are conceptually and strategically transformed and bundled through management processes into integrated strategic paths that can generate long-term net cash flow. However, this conceptual perspective is not usually that of many of the "techies" who inhabit and manage this world. This presents a major management challenge.

The New Product Functionality World

As shown in Figure 2.1, the world of new products, product functionalities, and buyer behavior represents the conceptual and physical transformation of bundles of physical technologies into specific bundles of differentiated end-customer and market network product functionalities. The end-user and market network adoption of these product functionalities is a perceptual, behavioral, and conceptual phenomenon, not just a physical phenomenon. End customers and market network members don't adopt products because of the technologies; they adopt them because of their perception of the differentiated and powerful competitive-functionalities performance attributes, the value they offer for your bundle, and their capacity to integrate your competitive bundle into their bundle. Your strategic path literally becomes part of theirs.

In the laptop example used previously, the product designers are concerned with product functionality: what users want to happen when they sit down and start hitting the keys and the mouse. For many laptops directed at different end-user market segments, this may not require the latest new technologies in the product bundle.

Bridging the Two Management Worlds: An Example

Bridging these two different worlds, both internally in companies and externally in competitive markets, is a major management-process problem facing technology-intensive companies today. It will continue to be so for a long time to come.

An excellent example of this bridging problem is Nortel's North American market entry with the Vantage key telephone system.[2] Vantage was a local telephone switching system for small businesses with up to one hundred local telephone handset users. In this case, the technologies bundle for the Vantage system was developed internally and largely independently by a separate team and company related to Nortel: Bell-Northern Research (BNR). It was a complex technology bundle since it had to integrate with both upstream and downstream digital-switching hardware and software. BNR was primarily a technology development and research organization, operating in the physical technologies world, focused entirely on developing, applying, and bundling the latest and "best" new telecommunications technologies, particularly digital technologies. BNR had successfully developed world-leading large digital switchgear for Nortel, which had created high positive net cash flows. Their culture and strategic choice processes clearly reflected the physical technologies world. For a particular individual technology need, they would frequently choose and bundle the latest, newest, and most exotic components, preferably ones that they had developed themselves.

As the technologies bundle for the key system developed and evolved over seven long years, it changed frequently, reflecting new and emerging individual technologies BNR had developed or adopted. Some provided useful and differentiated product functionalities, but some did not. These were not their prime criteria. Many of these new technology changes during the design process prolonged the developed time. This long development time, and its impact on competitive differentiation, proved to be a major problem later. Little focus was put on the specific technologies necessary to create the most important product functionalities for different end-user segments. The BNR technical staff worked little with other functional managers, including the critical manufacturing process managers.

For the new Vantage key system, the product functionalities bundle was entirely dictated and defined by the technologies bundle, rather than being strategically integrated during the development process. In this case, product functionalities represented what managers in small companies perceived they wanted in a telephone key system. As a result, the product was far too technically complex for the largest end-user segments, unreliable, and difficult for end users to understand and use. Little end-user research and product testing was done during the development period. The key system went directly from BNR development to Nortel manufacturing to the market.

The impact on the market networks was serious. In North America, these networks were run by telephone companies (telcos) and a large number of independent dealers. These companies already had access to many Asian key systems, which had much simpler and more reliable functionality at much lower prices. The technical complexity of the Nortel system had driven up their manufacturing costs, and therefore their prices were much higher than the Asian competitors. As a result of the product's overcomplexity and difficulty in-use for end users, telephone companies and dealers in the market network had high service, training, and inventory costs, which damaged their own net cash flow from the product. They had not been consulted during the development process.

Little focus was placed on any specific end-user company segments. The product was very high priced compared to the competition, without offering differentiated functionality. As a result the actual size of the viable end-user target segment was a fraction of the total market size.

The net cash flow estimates had assumed access to the entire North American key-system market. However, because of the high prices, they really had access to only a small segment of the market who might perceive the complex functionality as useful. Moreover, Nortel built an expensive, large-scale manufacturing plant in Canada to service the whole North American market. However, they had no real market network access into the United States market, where most of the unit potential was. The United States market was about ten times as large as Canada. The manufacturing investments and fixed costs caused a huge negative cash flow and made it impossible to hope for positive net cash flow from the strategic path.

The product had low adoption rates, failed, and suffered high negative net cash flow. In a sense, the whole development and marketing process reflected the polar opposite of the strategic-path concept. Each of the four critical strategic bundles was developed and managed separately, as if the others did not exist. Moreover, little concern was given to the net cash flow characteristics of the project. The two management worlds, and the critical strategic-path interactions they represent, were never integrated.

Looking at this management challenge, Burgelman, Maidique, and Wheelwright observed that,

> according to one school of thought, it is enough to understand the parameters transformed by the technological black box. That is, it is enough to know what the technological device or system does not how it does it. An alternative point of view argues that unless one understands the functioning of a device, and the laws that delineate its limitations, one cannot make effective judgments regarding the shaping of relevant technologies into successful products.[3]

MAJOR MANAGEMENT PROBLEMS

A major objective of the strategic-path processes outlined in this book is to bring together the managers from these two worlds into project and transformation teams and take them through a process that will enable them to transform new technologies into high net cash flow integrated strategic paths. The Nortel example, and many others similar to it, clearly outlines what can happen without this integration.

Lack of Market Focus

The lack of market focus has become an ongoing and more visible problem in many technology-intensive companies. Market focus has to take place in all four of the critical strategic-path choices: specific technology choices, specific product functionality choices, end-user segment choices, and market network choices. Market focus must also be integrated across all four strategic bundles. It is difficult to gain focus in any one of these areas, much less all of them.

Accomplishing strategically integrated focus in all four areas is extremely difficult and requires dramatically improved management processes. Roberts and Meyer have outlined the strategic importance of integrated market focus in both technologies and markets.[4] There is little doubt that for many companies the half-life of market-focused strategies is rapidly diminishing. For some companies, the technologies are rapidly changing. In other cases, the product functionalities change the fastest. It can also be the market networks that rapidly evolve. Finally, frequent churn in the nature of end-user segments and their needs can occur.

Integrating New Technologies Choices into Strategic-Market Planning

In the past few decades it has become clear that the competitive pressures have grown enormously for technology-intensive businesses. It is difficult to imagine any business that is not profoundly affected by the rate of change of new technologies. Similarly, it is hard to find a company that has not been influenced by the global competitive pressures arising from, in many cases, unsuspected and unpredictable new technologies.

We are surrounded by entire industries that have come from dramatically new and different technologies. As a result, huge step-function changes in the fundamental solutions to many customer needs have been made. New competitive companies have come forth in many industries that didn't exist before, and many companies have faded into obscurity as a result of not keeping up with the latest technologies.

As a result, the half-life of many competitive technologies has diminished significantly, whereas twenty years ago stable competitive strategies could have a half-life of five to ten years. Today, for many managers, such a thing as a stable competitive strategy no longer exists. Even the latest technologies will sometimes have a half-life of only six months to a year before a dramatically improved technological solution is developed. It is no longer an option, technologically, to stand still, either from a development or adoption point of view. Even in some of the most mundane industries globally, new technologies are having a dramatic impact.

Some current examples of "hot" new technologies are the following:

- Wireless networks and devices (Nortel, Research in Motion)
- Genetic and medical technologies, biotechnologies (genomics)
- Fuel cells (Ballard, Mercedes-Benz)
- Molecular and subatomic processes, nanotechnology, molecular engines
- Superconductivity
- Medical imaging (General Electric)
- Internet, intranet video, voice/data, distance learning (Microsoft)
- Organ transplants/replacement
- Semiconductors, chip technology (National Semiconductor, Motorola)
- Plastics, laminates, and adhesion technologies (3M)
- Batteries and electrical power systems
- Robotics, computer controls, computer-integrated manufacturing
- Photonics, lasers

- Artificial intelligence, fuzzy logic (IBM)
- Pharmaceuticals, health technologies (Novartis)

Each of these broad technology fields represents an enormous range, diversity, and variety of potential individual technologies and "bundles" of technologies. In many cases they approach the infinite in the permutations and combinations of technologies and product functionality they can produce. Companies and managers competing in these fields have a huge task in creating, managing, and sustaining market focus.

Measures of Success for New Products and Technologies

In looking at different companies' performances in integrating technologies into successful competitive strategies, a wide range of concepts and measures of success are seen, in many cases conflicting and contradictory. This has resulted in much confusion among many managers. Given today's competitive environment, a growing acceptance of the superordinance of net cash flow generation as the primary overall measure of success of corporate performance has occurred. This book will clearly embrace this point of view. The most important measure of long-term success for new technologies is the generation of high long-term net cash flow. The rationale for this will be outlined in detail.

Many other measures for new product and technology success are observed in companies, and often from the point of view of managers in different functional areas. Some examples of "success" measures are sales revenue, market share, rate of adoption of the technology and products, commercialization, return on investment, return on equity, EBITDA (earnings before interest, tax, depreciation, and amortization), and many others. Some of these are operational and measurable with real data, but many are not. More important, many of these measures are directly conflicting, and some can even look good even though negative net cash flow is the real outcome. All of the following examples have been observed in several companies:

- Sales revenue can be high, but can be accompanied by negative cash flow.
- Market share can also be high, but result in cash loss.

- Some companies claim a "commercialization success" when they sell one system, even though the overall result is a cash loss.
- Adoption rate can be significant, but a cash loss can still occur.

This book takes the clear position that no measure of success is relevant unless it results in the generation of high long-term positive net cash flow. This measure can be easily shown to outrank any of the other "better, valid" measures of success. Describing a new product and technology that has had a high adoption rate but negative net cash flow as a success would seem to be ridiculous.

Failure Rate for New Technologies and Products

The failure rate for new products and technologies is well documented for different technologies in different competitive marketplaces. All of the available data indicate that the failure rate is very high, but, as with defining success, the question of how you define "failure" is raised.

For this book, failure will not be defined only as technologies and products that don't make it to market, but, more important, as including those that do make it to market but generate negative or poor net cash flow. Conceptualized this way, it is likely that the real failure rate for new technologies and products is much higher than that cited in the literature because of the loose measures of success frequently used. The risks and cash flow problems facing the Nortel Vantage key system as well as companies developing car fuel cells have been outlined and discussed.

In the case of Biopure, the technologies of artificial blood (blood synthesized from bovine blood) will be featured.[5] Two distinct and very different potential strategic paths were possible: one for human application, the other for animals. In this case, end-user adoption on the animal strategic path has been slow, with poor net cash flow, and the human strategic path has still not been launched, with high cash losses. So far, the venture has been a failure.

Another interesting failure was that of the Zenith Minisport laptop computer.

> Probably the end of Zenith's short-lived laptop dominance. It used a combination backlit/reflected LCD which made the

screen hard to read in all conditions. Most everything was in ROM and the storage was on two inch floppy disks. That system unfortunately didn't work, despite a lot of hype that it was the future of floppy disk technology. The machine had all sorts of dubious features.[6]

This situation is a great example of an exciting and highly differentiated new technologies bundle creating a poor product functionalities bundle.

Seeing Failure As a Technology Problem Rather Than a Market-Focus Problem

An old cliché in technology-intensive businesses is, "It was a great product, but it failed," meaning that the technology did something exciting and unique but the product failed. The Zenith example illustrates this well. Frequently, the failure of a new technology-based product has far more to do with the entire strategy surrounding the technology and product rather than the product itself. The real cause of many new product and technology failures is a company's failure to integrate the choice of technologies with other critical strategic choices that drive success in the marketplace and high long-term net cash flow.

Another example of this problem is the current situation in the third-generation (3G) technology mobile-phone wireless networks markets.[7] In this case, the 3G technologies bundle was a huge step up in complexity from the 2G (second-generation) technology bundle for both the technology and potential product functionality. The technology requires companies to set up networks of huge complexity and cost. It was described as "the biggest ever gamble on the introduction of a new technology."[8] In dollar terms, mobile wireless companies globally invested about $125 billion (US). It was seen as a fabulous new technology, highly differentiated from the previous 2G technology bundle.

The resulting planned product functionality bundle seemed equally incredible, diverse, and universal. It was noted that

> the 3G will function as a phone, a computer, a pager, a videoconferencing centre, a newspaper, a diary, and even a credit card. . . . It will support not only voice communications

but also real time video and full-scale multimedia. It will automatically search the Internet for relevant news and information on pre-selected subjects, book your next holiday for you online, and download a bedtime story for your child, complete with moving pictures. It will even be able to pay for goods when you shop via wireless electronic funds transfer. In short the new mobile handset will become the single indispensable life tool carried everywhere by everyone, just like a wallet or purse is today.[9]

From a market network perspective, the new 3G technologies bundle was conceptualized as replacing the entire current bundles for all users, including telephony, as opposed to augmenting and replacing functionality for specific end-user segments. As a result, the different companies' market strategies had little market focus.

From an end-user segment perspective, little market focus occurred. In reality, the transformation for end-users to the new functionalities bundles was likened to "the evolution of television over the past forty years, from crude black and white to hundreds of digital channels in color. To expect customers to snap into this in five minutes is just unrealistic."[10] Furthermore, "the challenge for 3G companies is to understand the appeal of different services to different types of customers. That will require careful market segmentation. 3G gives you more scope, and segmentation broadly becomes more important."[11]

At this point, in net cash flow terms for the individual companies, the new 3G technologies are a clear failure. Some companies have returned their licences for which they paid huge cash sums.

Lack of Concepts and Processes for Evaluating New Technologies

A great need exists among corporate managers for easy-to-use and powerful processes and tools to help create focus for evaluation process for technologies and products. Many of the published processes and tools offered by both business schools and consultants are extraordinarily complex, situationally constrained, and in too many cases focus solely on irrelevant, homogeneous characteristics of the products without regard for choices of technologies, end-user segments, market networks, or their integration with the overall strategy.

Functional Isolation of Critical Technology and Related Strategic Choices

A recurring problem in many companies is the functional isolation of critical strategic choices on the strategic path. In many companies, choice of technologies, process manufacturing, sourcing, and products are made by R&D (research and development), engineering, and technical staff long before any integrated strategy is planned. Similarly, other critical choices in manufacturing, product design, and marketing and sales strategy are made at different points in time by different people.

As a result, integration of the competitive strategy planned for the technology never really takes place. What does take place is a fragmented process with conflicting objectives and criteria for success. As mentioned before, from an engineering and technical point of view, success is often seen as the mere fact that the technology functions in use.

One critical condition widely advocated is the use of multifunctional teams and the continuous involvement of these teams over the entire life cycle of the technology and product. In order for these multifunctional teams to work, all of the team members must understand the critical connections that have to be made when creating strategy. This is outlined in this book.

Stopping New Technology Projects in Process: The Avalanche Effect

In many companies, once resources and people's time have been committed to a new technology and product and it starts to take shape, it is extraordinarily difficult to stop the project, even when new information makes it clear that it is highly unlikely to ever achieve positive net cash flow. To exacerbate this "avalanche" effect realistic net cash flow estimates are often not made until quite late in the process. Many factors contribute to this effect. Some of them are as follows:

- The technologies in question can be the proprietary result of years of research, and simply "must" be applied.

- The management teams have few process checks and balances, have a lot of team commitment, and continue until it is too late to stop.
- Little or no communication occurs between the managers who choose the technologies, product functionalities, market networks, and end-user segments.
- Agreements have been made with specific customers that seem to prevent exit from the market.
- The technologies bundle is almost complete, and firm commitments have been made to suppliers.

Many other factors as well can cause this avalanche effect.

THE NEW TECHNOLOGY DEVELOPMENT-ADOPTION GAP

The huge growth in new technology development has resulted in challenging strategic development for many new technology-based companies. This technology development-adoption gap is shown in Figure 2.2. This gap profoundly affects not only individual firms, but explains much about the current slump in Nortel Networks and the entire market for wireless technology.

As shown, the global development rate of new technologies across the entire range of technologies is proceeding at an astronomic rate. In the past twenty years, the rate of development of new technologies in many areas has grown exponentially and at an increasingly accelerated rate. It is important to note that this is the growth of new physical technologies, not of their applications in product functionalities. At the same time, the individual and collective capacity of end users, companies, and market networks to absorb these technologies in the form of product functionalities is increasing at a much slower rate, depending on the situation.

For many reasons, end-use consumers, customer companies, and market networks cannot adopt new technology applications as quickly as they are developed. The result is a technology development-adoption gap: a fast growing gap between the rate of development of new technologies and the global capacity of markets to adopt them in the form of product functionality.

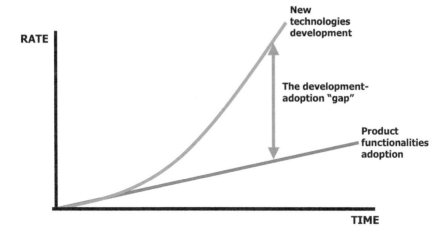

FIGURE 2.2. The new technologies development-adoption gap.

Among others, these phenomena are substantiated by Bettis and Hitt.[12] They note

> both the rate of technological change and the speed of technological diffusion have increased significantly in recent years. These two changes reinforce each other, and their effects cannot be easily separated. Greater speed of diffusion necessarily implies increased speed of technological change. Increased speed of change necessitates more rapid acquisition of relevant technologies by firms, and hence motivates diffusion-increasing behaviour.[13]

Technology Development and Adoption: New Product Adoption Curve versus the Technology S-Curve

Two unique and very different management worlds have been identified: the physical technologies world and the product functionalities world. These are directly connected to the development-adoption gap: the enormous gap between the rate of new technologies development and the rate of their adoption in terms of new products. In addition to the development-adoption gap, both worlds have a temporal characteristic to them in terms of their behavior over time.

New Technologies Development: The S-Curve

For the physical technologies world, new technologies are theoretically created and evolve along the well-known development curve shown in Figure 2.3. This curve has been characterized as the *S-curve,* but in fact the shape and nature of this wave are unique to the technology, and no easy generalization exists. Interpretations of the meaning of the S-curve vary widely. As shown, the rate of development of a new technology tends to be very rapid and in a growth phase at the beginning, and then begins to decline at some point in time in terms of physical changes in its applications. In some technologies the development wave can be very steep and fast; in other technologies it can be very flat and slow.

New Product Adoption Curves

The product/market world is represented by the *adoption curve,* which looks at the theoretical rate of market adoption of new product functionalities to arise from a technology. As shown in Figure 2.3, the adoption curve has a similar shape to the S-curve. In many cases, adoption tends to be more rapid at the beginning and to decline later, although, again, this is unique to the situation and cannot be generalized. As in the case of the technology S-curve, interpretation of the meaning of the adoption curve varies widely. Too often it is regarded

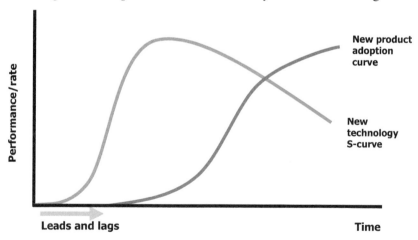

FIGURE 2.3. New product adoption curve versus new technology S-curve.

by managers as the norm for new products and a basis for sales forecasts. Nothing could be further from the truth. In reality, when applied to particular new product introductions, it seldom follows a predictable pattern. This will be outlined in Chapter 5.

Development and Adoption Interactions: The Battle of the Curves

Managing the interaction of these two complex, temporal phenomena is a major challenge in dealing with new technologies. Factors that complicate the way these two waves interact are the "leads and lags." For some end-user segments, the adoption curve can actually lead the S-curve with applications of the technology sought after and, in fact, self-developed by some companies and lead users. This phenomenon has been extensively outlined by von Hippel.[14] In other cases the S-curve leads the adoption curve by a significant period of time. Again, no convenient generality exists. It depends on the situation, the behavior of competing companies, and how the competitive situation is managed by all concerned.

One of the major challenges facing managers is understanding and analyzing the critical technologies required to produce the new product bundle from those technologies. The different technologies in the bundle could represent many different S-curves, with technologies at different stages of development. In competitive situations, both curves, and the relationship between the curves, must be clearly understood by managers, and their interpretations must be discussed and challenged.

Interesting examples of this phenomenon are disruptive technologies. These represent discontinuous S-curves, and are examples of situations in which emerging technologies require dramatic new strategic paths to exploit. Many companies faced with these opportunities fail to conceptualize this. Bower and Christensen noted that

> the pattern of failure has been especially striking in the computer industry. IBM dominated the mainframe market but missed by years the emergence of minicomputers, which were technologically much simpler than mainframes. Digital Equipment [Corporation] (DEC) dominated the minicomputer market

with innovations with its VAX [virtual address extension] architecture, but missed the personal computer market almost completely. Apple Computer led the world of personal computing and established the standard for user-friendly computing, but lagged five years behind the leaders in bringing its PC [personal computer] to market.[15]

Here we have companies not realizing that these new technologies require the conceptualization of entirely different strategic paths.

Implications for Managers

The new technology development-adoption gap represents huge challenges to managers in technology-intensive businesses. Managers in many companies will have many more choices of technologies to develop and adopt, and, in addition, more choices to bundle when developing product functionality. This is an enormous problem. Managers will have many permutations and combinations of technological bundles to put together for any particular product functionality solution. The management process of making technological choices will, therefore, become much more complex.

The increase in management decision-process complexity regarding technologies choices will drive the cost of developing and adopting the right product technologies increasingly higher as well. It simply takes much more time, money, and human-resource commitment to compare the choices of technologies bundles.

Faced with the increased number of technology choices, managers are going to have to make quicker yes-and-no decisions. Given the shorter strategic-path life cycles, managers will have to make faster decisions and move quickly to markets, exacerbating the risks. They are going to have to say no much more than yes to specific strategic-path choices.

This particular set of difficulties pertains to the choice of new technologies, but several other critical choices must be made concerning rapid change and complexity, including choices of product functionality, end-user segments, and which market networks will deliver the product functionality to those end users. These key competitive spaces all represent escalating choice difficulty.

Implications for the New Technologies and Product Development Processes

The new technologies and product development processes are shown in simplified form in Figure 2.4. As shown, new technologies go through three broadly defined, overlapping, temporally linked processes, each with great complexity and diversity in different company and organizational settings:

1. The pure research process
2. The applied research and development process
3. The new product development process

As managers, organizations, and technologies cycle through this complex set of processes over time, the technologies choices begin to narrow as fewer and fewer of them have the potential to become bundled into successful new product functionalities. The development-adoption gap represents an explosion of technology choices for many companies, both on the adoption and development side. In addition to an explosion in pure research and new technologies, an explosion of potential adopted technologies, and thus of technologies to bundle to create new products, has occurred. In many cases, the number of bundle permutations approaches infinity, therefore companies must make

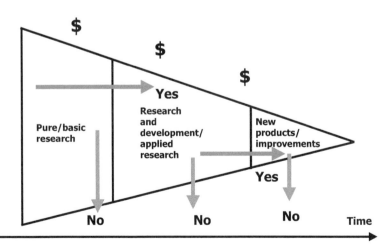

FIGURE 2.4. The new technologies development/evolution process.

more focused choices early on in the research phase as to how they will bundle technologies based on product functionality. Companies can be both developers and adopters of new technologies. In fact, some of the most successful new technology developers are also the most successful adopters. This demands that many choices be made earlier in the process.

Managers will have to be more skilled in process management because of the increase in technology development. The time line from pure research to specific new products can be years, and during this time it is important for managers to have a cohesive process for the choices they make. As noted earlier, managers in highly market-focused companies will have to say no much more often than yes to potential new technology and product opportunities. The percentage of opportunities they will have to decline will escalate rapidly. The organizational processes for choosing and rejecting new technology and product opportunities will have to become compressed in speed and focus.

Looking at Figure 2.4, managers and management teams have to be capable of saying no at every stage of the process: no to new research areas, no to R&D areas and applied research, and no to specific new products. Often this is not done, and once research gets under way it is carried through to a new product even when the evidence becomes clear that no possibility of positive net cash flow exists.

THE NEED FOR NEW MANAGEMENT PROCESSES, CONCEPTS, AND TOOLS

Thus far a management-process perspective has been outlined for managers dealing with the choices of new technologies and products to take to competitive markets. In the following chapters, the complexity of these processes will be expanded upon. Given the four major choices along the strategic paths, the challenges that teams of managers face in making these choices and making them turn into successful and profitable strategies are enormous. A great need exists for new management processes and concepts, as evidenced by the huge outpouring of books and articles on the topic over the past ten years. The processes and concepts that managers need most desperately are ones that they can integrate with their existing processes and use to raise additional and sharper questions, rather than to entirely replace their current process looking at new technology choices.

Managers need processes that are simple and easy to use, that are easy to understand and communicate, that can be used quickly, and that require minimal documentation. They need concepts that are consistent with the concepts they are currently using, because no one single, grand, overarching process model exists with which managers can manage new technologies and new products.

One of the key requisites for these new tools is to recognize the size of the array of choices of strategic-path bundles that managers face. Given this, tools are needed that will quickly allow managers and teams to explore a wide range of potential strategic paths through rapid iterations. That is a major objective of this book.

CRITICAL QUESTIONS FOR MANAGERS

- When you look at the strategic choices available for your current new technologies and products, what is your sense of your degree of market focus: the ability of your managers to clearly say yes and no?
- What is your sense of how focused your technologies are?
- What is your sense of how focused your product functionality choices are?
- What is your sense of how focused your choice of end-user segments is?
- What is your sense of how focused the market networks between you and your end-user segments are?
- In each one of these areas for market focus, who in your company exercises leadership and power with respect to making these choices? Where are the choices made and who makes them?
- Can you think of recent situations in which you clearly said no to a new technology, a new product, a new end-user segment, or a new market network member?
- What is your sense of how the four critical choices are integrated in your company?

- Who takes leadership for this integration, who has power, and what are the organizational mechanisms in place to do this effectively?
- When it is clear that you are going down a strategic path that is unlikely to produce positive net cash flow, how does your management team react?
- What kinds of explicit connections exist in your internal organization between the technologies world and the market world?
- What measures of financial success do you use for new technologies and new products?
  — Do they make sense against the criterion of net cash flow?
  — Are they operational and are they tough?
  — How often are they reviewed?
- Do you have well-defined processes in place to evaluate opportunities and to make sure they are reviewed on a continuing basis?

Chapter 3

Creating Focused Strategic Paths: Managing the Four Critical Bundles

INTRODUCTION

A strategic path describes the details of the critical set of four primal strategic bundles and competitive spaces that define market focus for a new technology and product situation. More important, managers must clearly set up the critical conditions necessary to integrate and create strategic synergies between the four bundles in order to create a highly competitive and cohesive market strategy. The four competitive spaces have been outlined as technologies, product functionalities, market networks, and end-user segments. These four areas for strategic choice drive and constrain the entire strategy for new technologies and products, and are the most instrumental strategic choices for the product's ultimate success.

The power of these strategic paths for managers exists on many levels. Most important, they allow teams of managers to achieve a planning-process focus that leads to market focus. Focusing on only four strategic bundles enables managers to gain analytic depth in these four areas and to really penetrate the impact of changes in any of the critical choices. This increase in analytic depth and focus helps managers and teams more effectively probe the six transformation processes in all their dimensionality and complexity.

It is important to note that companies do not have to compete or differentiate on all four strategic bundles. Some companies compete only in technologies, and thus market their technology's access and use by other companies using licensing and other mechanisms. Other companies compete only in product functionalities, outsourcing the technologies and market networks. Still other companies compete only in market networks by differentiating them and providing access to specific end-user segments. This is an exciting reality. It means that companies not only have the challenge of putting together competitive strategic paths, but also have the choice of areas of these paths on which create differentiation.

STRATEGIC PATHS AS COMPLEX STRATEGIC BUNDLES

As shown simply in Figure 3.1, strategic paths are, in fact, a set of four complex strategic bundles representing a very complex array of choices in each of the areas. These will now be outlined in detail with examples.

Examples

Three very different case examples of strategic paths will be used to illustrate the concept. These cases are situationally very different, with different sets of choices, yet the fundamental strategic choices are the same.

Medical Imaging

Medical imaging (Figure 3.2) offers an incredible array of potential strategic paths. Technologies alone, for example, General Electric and other companies such as Toshiba and Varian, represent a huge and growing inventory of potential imaging technologies, not to mention the enabling and peripheral technologies involved with the machines in hospital application, supply-side support, and market-side technologies. The potential use of X-ray, tomography, CAT (computerized axial tomography) scanning, magnetic resonance imaging (MRI), and nuclear scanning represent an incredible array of hardware, software, and controls available for the basic technologies choices. The number of alternative bundles of technologies alone available for strategic choice is staggering.

In bundling product functionalities in this field, the number of different scanning modalities and types of scans of various bodily tissues is enormous. A wide range of other product functionalities in use exists that hospitals and clinics need to explore when choosing an imaging machine and system.

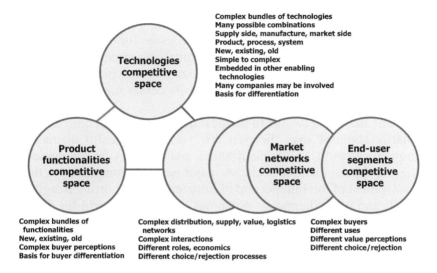

FIGURE 3.1. What is a strategic path? Strategic bundles.

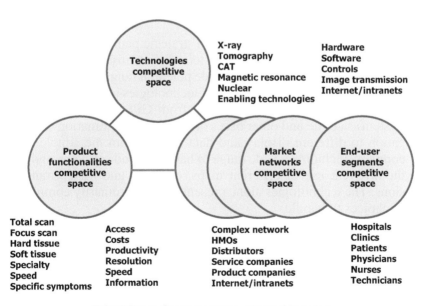

FIGURE 3.2. Strategic paths: Medical imaging.

For end-user segments, from hospitals to small private clinics, an enormous array of options exist representing dramatically different needs, usage, and choice/rejection processes for different technologies and product functionalities. Hospitals represent one of the most complex and difficult types of organizations to which to market and sell. Their choice, rejection, or usage processes for imaging is complex and unique at the hospital level.

The market networks in medical imaging have become extraordinarily complex over the past few years with health maintenance organizations (HMOs), distributors, and new service companies entering the competitive scene. A major network complexity is the involvement of the Internet and of intranets in transporting imaging results and other diagnostic outcomes all over the world for different radiologists and medical staff to explore.

Looked at as a strategic path, the medical imaging example is extraordinarily complex, within which companies such as General Electric, Toshiba, Varian, and many others have to create, integrate, and manage clear strategic paths to establish and sustain market focus. It is a huge management challenge.

Car Navigation Systems

Figure 3.3 shows some potential strategic paths for car navigation systems. These are navigation systems for car installation that determine direction, location, and a wide potential range of other information for the car driver. The range of technologies involved in potential technologies bundles is enormous, from GPS (Global Positioning System) satellite and other bases of location determination and navigation to different display and data media, from the simple to the complex, including a wide range of hardware and software, and from the different use of different maps, controls, and image transmissions. The technologies alone present an extraordinarily complex set of choices to bundle.

For product functionalities, different car navigation systems can perform a wide range of different functionalities, from the simple to the complex, including location, directions, and the nature of data display and the content. The media and data represent an enormous range of product functionality, including what information is displayed on the screen.

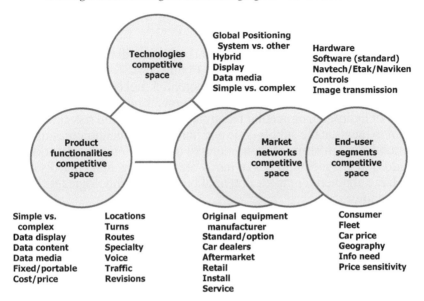

FIGURE 3.3. Strategic paths: Car navigation systems.

For end-user segments, all the way from company and rental fleets to individual consumers, different car prices and different types of vehicles, different geographies, different types of information, and price sensitivity, an enormous range of potential bundles of different segments exists. Each segment clearly requires very different product functionalities.

For market networks, an incredible array of choices exists, including installation by original equipment manufacturers (OEMs), aftermarket sales by car dealers and many other retailers, including choices regarding the roles of installation, service, and a wide range of roles for which the market network is responsible.

When you look at the number of permutations and combinations of potential strategic paths that a company such as Sony can choose for car navigation systems, it probably runs into the infinite. It is an outstanding example of the need for clear strategic-path management.

Fuel Cells

The last example to be cited in this section will be used extensively in this book, which is fuel cells (Figure 3.4). For the technologies competitive space a wide array of potential fuel cell technologies exist that are very different in their chemical reactions, performance, use of hydrogen, molecular reactions, emissions, and risks and safety, not to mention the supply-side and market-side technologies that surround them in terms of their potential use in different applications. In addition, the technologies of hardware, software, and controls add to a huge and very complex potential bundle of technologies for strategic choice.

For product functionalities, the same situation exists. Different fuel cells have very different functionality and performance in different applications, including horsepower, torque, operating costs, reliability, weight, and many other characteristics.

A huge range of potential end-user segments exist for fuel cells running from stationery and motive power sources, including the automotive segment, public transportation, and many others, with very different pricing and cost phenomena and characteristics.

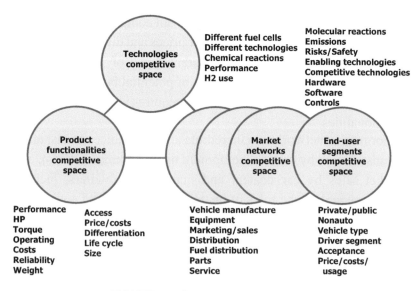

FIGURE 3.4. Strategic paths: Fuel cells.

The complexity of the market networks involved with fuel cells is extreme, including the manufacture of equipment and servicing of the fuel cells themselves, the manufacture and distribution of hydrogen or other fuel, and parts and service for the vehicles and surrounding technologies.

The fuel cells technologies and potential competitive markets present an enormously complex set of potential strategic paths within which companies such as Ballard and other fuel cell technology companies have to make clear choices of strategic paths. It is an extremely difficult and costly challenge.

A recent example of the enormous diversity of strategic paths for fuel cells is the application to industrial forklift trucks.[1] Clearly, the entire strategic path bundle for forklifts is very different than for car application or any other major application. A recent *Toronto Star* article points out, "it may not be as sexy as an exotic concept car, but a forklift truck powered by a hydrogen fuel cell could play an equally significant role in the march toward a hydrogen economy."[2] The report goes on to note that "industrial vehicles and their workplaces offer an ideal proving ground for fuel cell technologies."[3] In describing the product functionality bundle, the article notes, "their prolonged duty cycles, central fuelling infrastructure, and indoor use away from weather, permit rapid evaluation of reliability, durability, and performance."[4] In describing the technologies bundle, they note, "the overall efficiency of the electolyzer fuel-cell system is similar to that of the electric charger/battery system it replaces, but the fuel cell offers many other advantages."[5] In this application, it is important to note that the entire strategic path differentiates it from the car application, not just the technologies bundle.

TECHNOLOGIES COMPETITIVE SPACE: CHOICE OF TECHNOLOGIES BUNDLE

What do we mean by technologies? Although it seems straightforward, much debate occurs over different concepts of what "technology" means. This book clearly takes the position that technologies are physical, phenomenological, and molecular. They are physically real but, by themselves, are utterly useless. They are useful only when bundled with carefully focused and chosen other technologies to create functionalities bundles for products in terms of useful and competitively differentiated benefits from the customer's perception.

Bundling Technologies: Existing and New

We have conceptualized products as bundles of interconnected technologies. Laptops, for example, are interesting examples of bundles. Literally hundreds of different technologies are bundled and interconnected in such a way that they deliver a product functionality bundle. Some of the technologies in the bundle are old, some new, some exotic and highly differentiated, and some fairly mundane. As shown in Figure 3.5, a wide range of potential technologies bundles are possible. Managers can map any potential bundle on this map, and are likely to find that they face a large number of difficult strategic choices, some of which are constrained. For example, you might expect that the highest differentiation in most situations is in new technologies, but for laptops, it might be in the latest existing Intel microprocessor. Similarly, in certain situations, the differentiation for a new technology in the bundle might be low. Given a particular desired product functionality bundle in a specific situation, managers in competing companies could choose very different bundles of existing and new technologies.

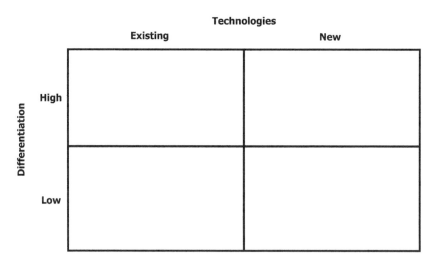

FIGURE 3.5. The technologies bundle: Existing and new.

Technologies are developed in physical processes, evolving and changing over time. They don't change simply from the point of view of new developments of technologies, but also in the ways they are adopted and bundled with other technologies to form product functionalities.

The Challenge of Premature Technologies

An interesting problem facing many companies is that of premature technologies: individual technologies that may produce an interesting phenomenological effect in isolation, but can't be bundled with other technologies in a way that creates highly differentiated product functionalities or allows the new technology to fulfill its potential (for example, putting a Ferrari engine in a dump truck). This raises the difficult issue of technologies timing, and many companies have discovered the hard way that bringing on technologies too quickly, bundled with other technologies, can produce no useful or differentiated product functionalities whatsoever. An interesting example is outlined by Kodama. Using the word *fusion* as a synonym for "bundling," he noted, "either a company can invest in R and D that replaces an older generation of technology, or it can focus on bundling existing technologies into hybrid technologies."[6]

Some examples of technologies bundling follow. FANUC, a leader in "mechatronics" in the 1970s, bundled electronic, mechanical, and materials technologies to develop an affordable computerized numerical controller (NC). Today, FANUC is the world leader in computerized NCs. Similarly, in the early 1980s, Sharp developed the first commercially viable liquid crystal display (LCD) for pocket calculators by bundling electronic, crystal, and optics technologies. Today, the company controls 38 percent of the worldwide LCD market, valued at more than $2 billion.

These examples illustrate that companies can choose to compete and differentiate their bundles in the technologies competitive space alone. Many companies develop new technologies and then license them out to other companies to bundle with their technologies to create product functionalities. This can be an extraordinarily successful strategy. Because a company competes only in the competitive space of technologies does not mean they are not on a strategic path. They simply choose to traverse that particular dimension of the path, relying on others to manage the transformation processes with the other three paths. When looking at new technologies for a particular opportunity, therefore, it is critical to map the possible technology bundles, not just the particular technology.

Bundling Technologies: Adoption and Development

Another critical aspect of technologies bundling on a strategic path is the choice of adopted or developed technologies. Most new products of any complexity are bundles of both types. As Robertson pointed out, almost every large, sophisticated company now has a continuing program for evaluating and acquiring potentially useful technologies from outside.[7] Many different potential technologies bundles are possible, as shown in Figure 3.6. Here again, faced with a target product functionalities bundle, managers have a wide range of mixes of these four types of technologies.

Once again, no strategic generalities exist. However, strategic risks will arise from some choices. For example, in some situations, greater competitive advantage results when the highest technology differentiation comes from developed rather than adopted technologies. However, other factors drive the choice of the adopted technology. Similarly, in certain situations it may make sense to include low-differentiation developed technologies in the bundle.

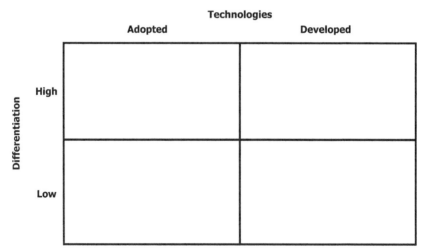

FIGURE 3.6. The technologies bundle: Developed and adopted.

Mapping the Technologies Space

As previously shown, strategic paths represent a huge diversity of technology choices and ways of bundling these choices. Teams of managers need to carefully and iteratively map the technologies space and explore how different technologies can be bundled together. Figure 3.7 shows the basis for such a map. In this map, the individual technologies in the bundle are organized on two important dimensions. One dimension is the importance of that technology to the product functionality bundle. A critical measure of this importance is the capacity of the technology to create competitive-functionality differentiation. This dimension is mapped against the degree of differentiation of the individual technology. What you are looking for on this map are individual technologies that are both important to the functionality solution and highly differentiated. These constitute a competitively powerful part of the functionality bundle.

The Fuel Cells Example

As outlined earlier, fuel cells represent an enormously complex technologies bundle, and will be used to illustrate these important

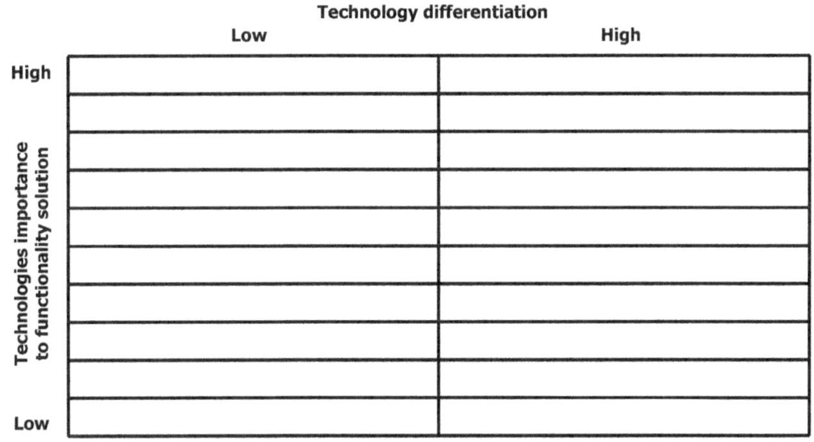

FIGURE 3.7. Mapping the technologies competitive space.

points.* In principle, a fuel cell operates similar to a battery. Unlike a battery, though, a fuel cell does not run down or require recharging. It will produce energy in the form of electricity and heat as long as fuel is supplied. A fuel cell consists of an electrolyte sandwiched between two electrodes. Oxygen passes over one electrode and hydrogen over the other, generating electricity, water, and heat. A fuel cell system that includes a "fuel reformer" can utilize the hydrogen from any hydrocarbon fuel, from natural gas to methanol and even gasoline. Since the fuel cell relies on chemistry and not combustion, emissions from this type of a system are much smaller than emissions from the cleanest fuel-combustion processes.

A wide array of different technologies choices are available for fuel cells, and, furthermore, a great number of choices exist within each of the different technologies. It is important to discuss these choices in detail to really drive the point home about the technologies world and its complexity and about the number of technology bundles available to choose from.

Fuel Cells Technology Choices

A large number of different fuel cell technologies exist, representing vastly different technology bundles. We will outline a few of these technologies to demonstrate. The critical fact here is that a company in this business must bring focus to their fuel cells technologies bundle at some point. It would be easy for a company to develop a particular fuel cell technology that serves one strategic path, but not one in which the best potential markets are.

It is important to outline these technologies in some detail to emphasize the huge physical differences between them. When managers choose to focus on one specific fuel cell technology they cannot just switch to another if they recognize the futility of its strategic path. The technologies choice has to be transformed into a coherent strategic path as soon as possible in the development process. At the same time, managers must be prepared to constantly challenge and change strategic paths.

Phosphoric acid technology. Phosphoric-acid fuel cells are commercially available today. Many of these fuel cell systems have been

---

*The information on fuel cells in this book is extensively quoted or abstracted from the Web site <www.fuelcells.org>, The Online Fuel Cell Resource, 2004.

installed all over the world, in hospitals, nursing homes, hotels, office buildings, schools, utility power plants, airport terminals, landfills, and wastewater treatment plants. These cells generate electricity at more than 40 percent efficiency, and nearly 85 percent of the steam this fuel cell produces is used for cogeneration. This compares to about 35 percent for the utility power grid in the United States. The electrolyte is liquid phosphoric acid. One of the main advantages to this type of fuel cell, besides the high efficiency, is that it can use impure hydrogen as fuel.

Proton exchange membrane technology. Proton-exchange fuel cells operate at relatively low temperatures (about 175°F), have high power density, can vary their output quickly to meet shifts in power demand, and are suited for such applications as in automobiles, for which quick start-up is required. They are the primary candidates for light-duty vehicles, for buildings, and potentially for much smaller applications such as replacements for rechargeable batteries. The proton-exchange membrane is a thin plastic sheet that allows hydrogen ions to pass through it. The membrane is coated on both sides with highly dispersed metal alloy particles (mostly platinum) that are active catalysts. The electrolyte used is a solid organic polymer polyperfluorosulfonic acid. The solid electrolyte is an advantage because it reduces corrosion and management problems. This type of fuel cell is, however, sensitive to fuel impurities.

Molten carbonate technology. Molten-carbonate fuel cells use a liquid solution of lithium, sodium, and/or potassium carbonates. They promise high fuel-to-electricity efficiencies, about 85 percent with cogeneration, and operate at about 1,200°F. The high operating temperature is needed to achieve sufficient conductivity of the electrolyte. Because of this high temperature, noble metal catalysts are not required for the cell's electrochemical oxidation and reduction processes. To date, these have been operated on hydrogen, carbon monoxide, natural gas, propane, landfill gas, marine diesel, and simulated coal gasification products. They have been tested on a variety of fuels and are primarily targeted to electric utility applications.

Carbonate fuel cells for stationary applications have been successfully demonstrated in Japan and Italy. The high operating temperature serves as a big advantage because this implies higher efficiency and the flexibility to use more types of fuels and inexpensive catalysts since the reactions involving breaking of carbon bonds in larger hydrocarbon fuels occur much faster as the temperature is increased. A disadvantage to this, however, is that the high temperatures enhance corrosion and the breakdown of cell components.

Solid oxide technology. Solid oxide is another highly promising fuel cell that could be used in big, high-power applications, including industrial and large-scale central electricity generating stations. Some developers also predict its use in motor vehicles, and are developing fuel cell auxiliary power units with them. A solid oxide system usually uses a hard ceramic material of solid zirconium oxide and a small amount of yttrium instead of a liquid electrolyte, allowing operating temperatures to reach 1,800°F. Power-generating efficiencies could reach 85 percent with cogeneration, and cell output is up to 100 kW. Tubular designs are closer to commercialization and are being produced by several companies around the world.

Alkaline technology. Long used by NASA on space missions, alkaline cells can achieve power generating efficiencies of up to 70 percent. They were used on the Apollo spacecraft to provide both electricity and drinking water. Their operating temperature is about 400°F. They use an aqueous solution of alkaline potassium hydroxide. This is advantageous because the cathode reaction is faster in the alkaline electrolyte, which means higher performance. Until recently they were too costly for commercial applications, but several companies are examining ways to reduce costs and improve operating flexibility. They typically have a cell output from up to 5 kW.

Direct methanol technology. Methanol cells use a polymer membrane as the electrolyte. The anode catalyst itself draws the hydrogen from the liquid methanol, eliminating the need for a fuel reformer. Efficiencies of about 40 percent are expected with this type of fuel cell, and would typically operate at a temperature of about 190°F. This is relatively low, making this fuel cell attractive for tiny to midsized applications, for example, to power cellular phones and laptops. Higher efficiencies are achieved at higher temperatures. A major problem, however, is fuel crossing over from the anode to the cathode without producing electricity. Many companies have claimed to have solved this problem, however. They are working on prototypes used by the military for powering electronic equipment.

Regenerative technology. Regenerative fuel cells are attractive as a closed-loop form of power generation. Water is separated into hydrogen and oxygen by a solar-powered electrolyzer. The hydrogen and oxygen are fed into the fuel cell, which generates electricity, heat, and water. The water is then recirculated back to the solar-powered electrolyzer, and the process begins again. These types of fuel cells are currently being researched by NASA and others worldwide.

Zinc-oxygen technology. A typical zinc-oxygen fuel cell contains a gas diffusion electrode, a zinc anode separated by electrolyte, and some form of mechanical separators. A permeable membrane allows atmospheric oxygen to pass through. After the oxygen has converted into hydroxyl ions and water, the hydroxyl ions travel through an electrolyte and reach the zinc anode. Here it reacts with the zinc and forms zinc oxide. This process creates electrical potential. When a set of cells are connected, the combined electrical potential of these cells can be used as a source of electric power.

Companies are working on these cells that contain a zinc "fuel tank" and a zinc refrigerator that automatically and silently regenerates the fuel. In this closed-loop system, electricity is created as zinc and oxygen are mixed in the presence of an electrolyte, creating zinc oxide. Once the fuel is used up, the system connects to a grid and the process is reversed, leaving once again pure zinc fuel pellets. The key is that this reversing process takes only a few minutes to complete, so the battery recharging time is not an issue. The chief advantage zinc-oxygen technology has over other battery technologies is its high specific energy, which is a key factor that determines the running duration of a battery relative to its weight.

Protonic ceramic technology. Protonic ceramic fuel cells are based on a ceramic electrolyte material that exhibits high protonic conductivity at elevated temperatures. These cells share the thermal and kinetic advantages of high temperature operation with molten carbonate and solid oxide fuel cells, and exhibit all of the intrinsic benefits of proton conduction in polymer electrolyte and phosphoric acid fuel cells. The high operating temperature is necessary to achieve very high electrical fuel efficiency with hydrocarbon fuels. These cells can operate at high temperatures and electrochemically oxidize fossil fuels directly to the anode. This eliminates the intermediate step of producing hydrogen through a costly reforming process. Gaseous molecules of the hydrocarbon fuel are absorbed on the surface of the anode in the presence of water vapor, and hydrogen atoms are efficiently stripped off to be absorbed into the electrolyte, with carbon dioxide as the primary reaction product.

PRODUCT FUNCTIONALITIES COMPETITIVE SPACE: CHOICE OF FUNCTIONALITIES BUNDLE

What do we mean by product functionalities? Just as products are bundles of technologies, they are also bundles of functionalities. But whereas technologies are a physical bundle, product functionalities are a buyer and customer "perceptual" bundle. The laptop computer is a good example. When you look at the hardware and software capability of laptops and their use you are seeing a complex, multidimensional bundle of product functionalities. Different end users of laptops use different bundles of functionality from the same physical laptop, and can have very different perceptions of their value and competitive differentiation.

What is meant by product functionality differentiation? Given that products are bundles of functionalities, some of their functionalities will be differentiated from competitive products, and some will not. Several important dimensions of functionalities differentiation exist.

- First, functionalities should be compared to a specific competitive product, as opposed to a general product category. It should be a competitive bundle that the end-user segment sees as their best choice.
- Second, functionalities should represent useful, powerful product performance characteristics in the perception of the end user.
- Third, differentiation is based on the end user's performance criteria and perception, not on your or your manager's perception. It is critically important that differentiation be defined, conceptualized, and measured through the eyes of the customer, not those of the managers developing the product. Numerous examples exist of companies who thought they had highly differentiated product functionality for new technologies that was not perceived by end users.
- Finally, differentiation must form the basis for buyer choice and rejection of competitive products. Differentiation that does not drive buyer choice and rejection is not real differentiation. A critical issue here is that high technologies differentiation does not necessarily mean high product functionalities differentiation. In fact, many examples exist of highly differentiated technologies that led to negatively differentiated products.

The important strategic step when looking at product functionality competitive space is to map the possible product functionality bundles by end-user segment. Each segment will look to different bundles of functionalities for differentiation, and each must be specially recognized.

Mapping the Product Functionalities Space

Similar to mapping the technologies space, product functionalities space represents a huge range of potential differentiated product functionality dimensions for different end-user segments. Figure 3.8 illustrates one map to use to explore which product functionality attributes will have the greatest differentiating capability. This map plots two critical dimensions of product functionality. The first dimension is the functionality importance to the solution, which represents the specific functionalities that are most central and critical to the end-use customer. The second dimension is competitive functionality differentiation, which represents the degree to which each functionality dimension is differentiated from your best competitor. What you are looking for here is functionality dimensions that are critical to the solution and have very high competitive differentiation.

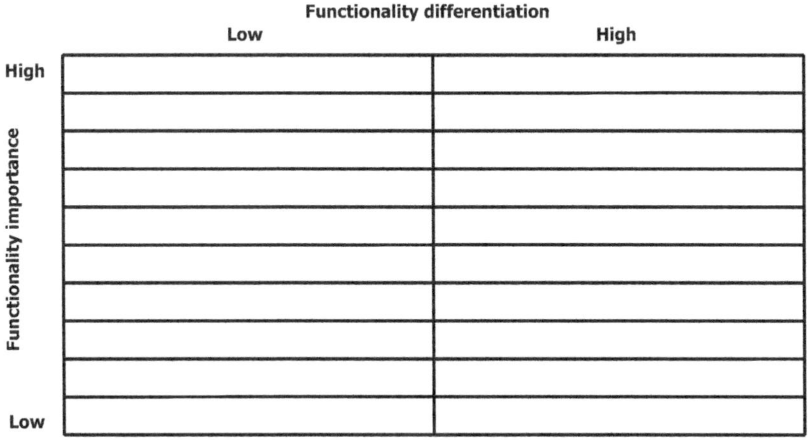

FIGURE 3.8. Mapping the functionalities competitive space (S2).

The Fuel Cells Example

Fuel cells present a huge array of potential product functionalities for different end-user segments. Some of these functionality attributes are discussed in the following sections.

Energy Security Functionality

United States energy dependence is higher today than it was during the "oil shock" of the 1970s, and oil imports are projected to increase. In the United States, passenger vehicles alone consume 6 million barrels of oil every single day, equivalent to 85 percent of all oil imports. If just 20 percent of cars used fuel cells, the United States could cut oil imports by 1.5 million barrels every day.

Supply Security Functionality

Because they are efficient, modular, and fuel flexible, fuel cells can enable a transition to a secure, renewable energy future, based on the use of hydrogen. A fuel cell system that includes a "fuel reformer" can utilize the hydrogen from any hydrocarbon or alcohol fuel, natural gas, ethanol, methanol, propane, or even gasoline or diesel. Hydrogen can also be produced from electricity from conventional, nuclear, or renewable sources.

Hydrogen can be extracted from novel feedstocks such as landfill gas or anaerobic digester gas from wastewater treatment plants, from biomass technologies, or from hydrogen compounds containing no carbon, such as ammonia.

Electrolysis uses an electric current to extract hydrogen from water. Fuel cells, in combination with solar or wind power or any renewable source of electricity, offer the promise of a zero-emission energy system that requires no fossil fuel and is not limited by variations in sunlight or wind flow. This hydrogen can supply energy for power needs and for transportation.

Physical Security Functionality

Because of their distributed nature, fuel cells could allow the United States to move away from reliance on central-station power generation, and long-distance, high-voltage power grids, which are likely terrorist targets in any attempt to cripple the energy infrastructure.

Reliability Functionality

Fuel cells can be configured to provide backup power to a grid-connected customer should the grid fail. They can also be configured to provide completely grid-independent power, or use the grid as the backup system. Modular installation (the installation of several identical units to provide a desired quantity of electricity) provides extremely high reliability. In specialized applications, fuel cells can achieve up to 99.9 percent reliability, less than one minute of down time in a six-year period.

Quality Power Functionality

Fuel cells offer high-quality power, which is crucial to the United States economy that depends on increasingly sensitive computers, medical equipment, and machines.

Efficiency Functionality

Because they make energy electrochemically and do not burn fuel, fuel cells are fundamentally more efficient than combustion systems.

Power Generation Functionality

Fuel cell power generation systems in operation today achieve 40 percent fuel-to-electricity efficiency utilizing hydrocarbon fuels. Systems fueled by hydrogen consistently provide 50 percent efficiency. Even more efficient systems are under development. In combination with a turbine, electrical efficiencies can exceed 60 percent. When waste heat is put to use for heating and cooling, overall system efficiencies exceed 85 percent.

Transportation Functionality

Fuel cells can help the United States move away from the current dependence on petroleum by providing more efficient vehicles in the short term and ultimately by allowing a transition to renewable energy. Fuel cell passenger vehicles are expected to be up to three times more efficient than internal combustion engines.

Environmental Functionality

Air pollution continues to be a primary health concern in many countries. Exposure to ozone, particulate, or airborne toxic chemicals has substantial health consequences. Scientists are now directly linking air pollution to heart disease, asthma, and cancer. Recent health studies suggest polluted urban air is a health threat comparable to passive smoking. Fuel cells can reduce pollution today and offer the promise of eliminating pollution tomorrow.

Fuel cells offer excellent environmental performance compared to power generation technologies that rely on combustion. Based on measured data, a fuel cell power plant may create less than one ounce of pollution per 1,000 kilowatt-hours of electricity produced, compared to the 25 pounds of pollutants for conventional combustion generating systems. Fuel cell power plants are so low in emissions that some areas of the United States have exempted them from air permit requirements, and fuel cell vehicles are the least polluting of all vehicles that consume fuel directly.

Fuel cell vehicles operating on hydrogen stored onboard the vehicles produce zero pollution in the conventional sense. Neither conventional pollutants nor greenhouse gases are emitted. The only by-products are water and heat. Systems that rely on an onboard reformer to convert a liquid fuel to hydrogen produce small amounts of emissions, but would still reduce smog-forming pollution by up to 90 percent compared to traditional combustion engines, depending on the choice of fuel.

The simple reaction that takes place inside the fuel cell is highly efficient. Even if the hydrogen is produced from fossil fuels, fuel cell vehicles can reduce emissions of carbon dioxide, a global warming concern, by more than half. Tests performed on a fuel cell bus fueled by methanol showed zero emissions of particulate matter and hydrocarbons, and near-zero emissions of carbon monoxide and nitrous oxides—levels far below the 1998 United States emission standard for buses.

Fuel cells used as auxiliary power units (APUs) to power air conditioners and accessories in over-the-road trucks could reduce emissions by up to 45 percent in long-haul vehicles and deliver economic benefits to the truck owner through lower fuel use and less wear and tear. According to the United States DOE, fuel cell APUs in Class 8 trucks can save 670 million gallons of diesel fuel per year and 4.64 million tons of carbon dioxide emission per year.

International Functionality

Fuel cells are entering the market at a time when countries face growing pressure to adopt alternative energy technologies on a large scale. The challenge for the fuel cell industry is to ensure that it is ready with competitively priced, performance-proven products as demand grows. More nations are focused on sustainable energy strategies. Fuel cells offer an opportunity for countries to move toward greater sustainability in resource consumption. Fuel cell efficiencies yield substantial reductions in emissions of climate-change gases and promise an end to the exclusive reliance on carbon fuels for energy.

Portable Power Functionality

Portable power applications cover a wide range of market segments, including small generators and battery replacements. Fuel cells are an excellent source of power for emergency and recreational uses for which access to the electric grid is not available. Domestic-generator-type products are currently nearing commercialization. Portable devices offer great potential as backup power supplies.

Fuel cell power sources are also being developed for portable electronic devices. In these applications, the fuel cell would provide a much longer operating life than would a battery, in a package of lighter or equal weight per unit of power output. The fuel cell would not require recharging—a liquid, solid, or gaseous fuel canister could be replaced in a moment. Fuel cells also have an environmental advantage over batteries since certain kinds of batteries require special disposal treatment. Fuel cells provide a much higher power density, packing more power in a smaller space.

The engineering and materials challenges related to micro fuel cell applications are substantial and will require innovative solutions to bring them to commercialization. If these technologies can be commercialized, then the portable and micro application market could be the fastest to develop. A huge potential market exists.

Portable fuel cells carry environmental benefits comparable to fuel cells in other applications to the extent they replace combustion systems in homes, in business, or in recreation. Fuel cells also carry productivity benefits in an increasingly mobile economy. Allied Business Intelligence's "Report on Portable Fuel Cells Markets," says portable fuel cells are being developed to respond to the "poor performance of rechargeable batteries by quadrupling the run time before refuelling is necessary."[8] Developers expect a fuel cell powered cell phone to have up to 200 hours of talk time. Recharging fuel cell powered electronic devices could be as simple as inserting a small methanol fuel cartridge or hydrogen container.

Military Functionality

Fuel cells could help the military reduce the cost of battlefield logistics, provide a source of energy for the modern soldier, save money, and reduce pollution at military installations, on board ships, and terrestrial vehicles. Most important, fuel cells could save lives and materiel by reducing telltale heat and noise. Stationary fuel cells are helping the military address their peak electric power needs while complying with the need to reduce energy use at federal facilities. Stationary fuel cells for military applications can provide backup or standby power for special operations and activities and can provide power in remote areas. Fuel cells may also provide life-saving power for the soldier of the future, who will be carrying enough electronic equipment to require one kilowatt or more of electric power.

Summary

It is important to acknowledge the huge range of potential product functionalities for fuel cells. The different functionalities do not all apply to all of the unique fuel cell technologies. Clearly, the transformation of the right technologies into the right functionalities takes on great importance for companies.

MARKET NETWORKS COMPETITIVE SPACE: CHOICE OF MARKET NETWORKS BUNDLE

What do we mean by market networks? Market networks conceptually encapsulate all of the distribution channels, supply chains, value chains, physical and virtual networks, and internets and intranets. They are, literally, the entire, complex web of physical, logistical, production, and information flows, virtual and physical, that surround the company when moving a product into the marketplace. These flows can be on both the supplier side and end-user side of the company and, in fact, managing the supplier side of the market chain is often as important as managing the end-user side. Market networks can be extremely long and complex. For example, semiconductors can be used in a wide range of high-technology electronic products. By their nature, market networks are difficult to create, manage, control, and plan. Numerous choices exist when looking at market networks and they evolve and change constantly.

One of the most difficult aspects of choosing, planning, and managing market networks is the complex relationships that exist among and between them. Indeed, complex market networks, such as those for semiconductors, involve a huge number of relationships, including virtually all of the real information and movement of the product.

In addition, in various competitive market situations many different market networks exist that can contact myriad end-user segments. Again, laptops are an excellent example of this. A large number of market networks reach different end-user segments. A good example of a highly differentiated market network is Dell Computers.

As with technologies competitive space, a company can choose to compete and differentiate itself in market networks competitive space alone, and can have a strategic path based on this area alone. Distributors take this position without competing in technologies, product functionalities, or end-user segmentation. When planning the strategic paths around market networks it is critical to map the possible market networks to different end-user segments.

Mapping the Market Networks Space

Market networks have been recognized as extraordinarily complex factors in competitive marketplaces. It is very important to map the possible market networks. One concept for mapping them is shown in Figure 3.9. As shown, the market network is mapped on two critical dimensions. The first dimension is the market networks potential. To develop this dimension, the leading market networks have to be mapped to include all of their major members. Their potential reflects estimates of the net cash flow potential for the products through that market network. This dimension is mapped against the second dimension: end-user segment potential. This represents the relative size of different end-user segments for the product. What you are looking for here is market networks that fit with the highest potential end-user customers segments.

The Fuel Cells Example

The Market Networks Space

A simple version of the market network space for fuel cells is shown in Figure 3.10. As shown, even in its simple form, a fuel cells market network bundle represents an incredible array of potential choices and permutations and combinations of bundles. Even within each of the individual members of the market network a huge array of choices exist. These individual members of the market network for fuel cells will be briefly described in the following section.

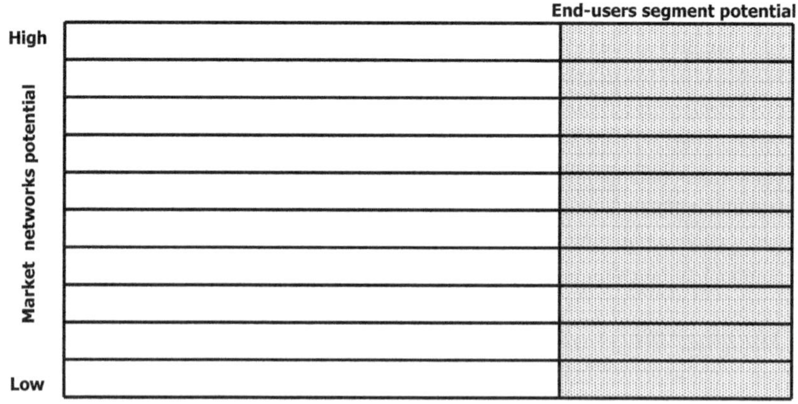

FIGURE 3.9. Mapping the market networks competitive space.

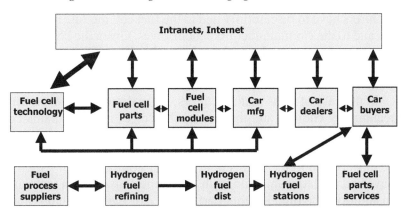

FIGURE 3.10. Fuel cells market networks: Cars.

Fuels Cell Technology Developers

In the fuel cells market network, technology developers may exist as separate members or they may be combined with other members. These companies who do research and development, such as Ballard Power Systems, develop the physical technologies to licence and sell in joint ventures with other companies in the market network. For companies such as this, the strategic choice of technologies is absolutely critical. Given the wide range of potential physical technologies, the issue of market focus is critical. Research and development for the technology is extremely expensive, and a problem facing these companies is that the choice of technologies is often tied more to the funding source than it is to their potential to form strategic paths downstream.

Fuel Cell Parts Manufacturers

Fuel cells parts manufacturers come into play when a strategic path is contemplated in which parts manufacturers are needed to provide parts to companies who put together manufacturing-level modules, which in this case go into cars as the power source. Parts manufacturers have to start planning these strategic paths long before specific cars get manufactured, and the design cycle for the cars' parts manufacturers have to be carefully tied to the fuel cell module manufacturers and to the car manufacturers themselves. Given the complexity of the technologies involved, the relationship between parts manufacturers, module manufacturers, and car manufacturers has to be extremely well-managed and focused.

In the case of parts manufacturers, it is easy to see how the wrong technology choices and the wrong choices of strategic paths could lead to major problems with fuel cell module manufacturers and car manufacturers. The parts manufacturers' choice of technologies will be closely tied to the fuel cell technology company with which they have had a relationship and from which they have gotten technology. In addition, the functionality performance of fuel cells in use may be quite different from that hypothesized by fuel cell technology developers. Fuel-cell parts companies have their own unique set of strategic paths they have to choose, but clearly they must be integrated with strategic paths upstream and downstream.

Fuel Cell Module Manufacturers

Fuel cell module manufacturers can be tier one (first level) suppliers to the car industry who will provide the integrated fuel cell power sources for installation in cars. In some cases, these manufacturers may be backward-integrated companies owned by the car companies. In this case, the companies must be on very clearly defined strategic paths involving very specific choices of technologies and product functionalities. Fuel cells are major financial commitments, and design of a poorly focused strategic path in terms of the physical technology could have disastrous consequences. These tier one module manufacturers should be in close contact with the car companies, and it is likely that technology and functionality choices will be specified by the car manufacturers. This is not always the case. For example, the internal combustion business contains many suppliers of gasoline powered combustion car engines that are not directly related to car manufacturers but sell engines on the open market. In this case, the choice of a bad strategic path could result in no engine sales.

Similarly, the fuel cell module manufacturers have to be sure of all the reliability and serviceability dimensions of the fuel cells they manufacture because they will be responsible for the downside if major problems occur in their use in cars. In some cases, some aspects of their strategic path choices may be in conflict with the fuel cell parts manufacturers, and indeed, the car manufacturer.

Car Manufacturers

Car manufacturers globally are in a highly competitive situation, for example, General Motors, Ford, Chrysler, Honda, Toyota, Nissan, and a wide range of others. Industry overcapacity is a continuing problem for many end-user segments. Fuel cells strategic paths are very contentious right now for any car maker, not in terms of whether fuel cells can be technically applied in some cars but whether any long-term net cash flow can be created by the car companies in using them. That is the real question. This brings into stark relief the importance of connecting strategic paths to real net cash flow. This is true of all companies and members of the market network, but especially true of car manufacturers. Numerous horror stories exist in the car industry of technological choices that have been made that were unmanageable by the market network and have resulted in significant losses when these technologies were installed in cars and the cars were subsequently attempted to be marketed. To actually pursue a strategic path involving fuel cells is an enormous gamble for a car company.

In addition to this, as fuel cell research and development have proceeded, development work on other alternative power sources has not been standing still, such as gasoline, diesel, electric, and hybrids such as gasoline-electric, diesel-electric, and others. Some of these share the performance differentiation of fuel cells, such as low emissions and high fuel economy. As the performance of the alternative power sources improves over time, much of the fuel cell differentiation could evaporate. The longer it takes for fuel cells to be applied, the more this will happen. The risks are escalating.

Car Dealers

One of the most interesting parts of the market network involving fuel cells is the car dealers who retail cars to end consumers. The dilemmas they face with the fuel cell strategic path are critical. Some segments of car buyers will be receptive and open to the differentiation offered by fuel cells and others will not. Some will accept, and others will reject. The critical issue of the net cash flow of fuel cell cars to dealers will be central. A very complex situation surrounds car dealers' willingness to adopt the fuel cell strategic path and to represent it as something they would like their car buyers to seriously consider. In their case, they have to represent all of the strategic paths that car manufacturers pursue. They have to be able to deal with the technology in service and understand and explain it to their sales reps and their service people. Dealers have to deal with differences in the functionality and performance of fuel cell cars as compared to ordinary internal combustion cars. They have to understand the different segments of car buyers who may or may not be receptive to fuel cell technology in their personal cars. This is critical, since the ultimate adoption of fuel cell cars can only happen at the dealer.

Car Buyers

Car buyers are a critical part of the market network, perhaps the most critical part. It is they who will ultimately choose or reject the strategic path pursued by car manufacturers with fuel cells. In that highly competitive market reality, it is likely that a large segment of car buyers may be unwilling or uninterested in buying and driving fuel cell–powered cars. The segmentation of car buyers is complex. Many different segments exist, some of which could be hostile to fuel cell technology, others simply unmoved, and others who would be very receptive. The big question is, how big are the different segments?

To make matters even more complicated, many consumers are not knowledgeable and are in a confused state about the attributes of all of the functionalities offered by alternative technologies. Large segments of the car market are naïve, suspicious, and uninterested in new technologies.

Fuel Process Suppliers

At the beginning of the market network for the availability of fuel for fuel cell powered cars, whether the fuel is hydrogen, methane, gasoline, or other, are the fuel process suppliers. These companies will be involved in the technologies that will provide and distribute the necessary fuel for the particular fuel cells. This is a crucial part of the market network because, depending on the particular fuel cell technology involved, the fuel requirements are quite different. Companies that build the process to produce the appropriate fuel and sell these processes to hydrogen fuel refining companies are critically important. They need to know, obviously, how the strategic paths of the fuel cells themselves look so they can provide the appropriate fuel. Since the design cycle for fuel process suppliers is very long, fuel-producing companies have to start going down their strategic paths relatively soon compared to the development of viable fuel cells in cars. What companies are going to do this?

Hydrogen Fuel Refining

Hydrogen fuel refining refers to the massive manufacturing facilities that will be required to produce the hydrogen, methanol, or other type of fuel required to power car fuel cells. Clearly, the decisions to put together processes and to build facilities to produce hydrogen fuel will come significantly after the commitment to the strategic path by fuel cell technology firms and fuel cell parts manufacturers. The investments in the hydrogen fuel refining could be very high since the cycles for designing and building the processes along with locating them could be significantly long. The type of fuel and the characteristics of the fuel will be very contingent upon the fuel cell technologies that become part of the strategic paths.

Hydrogen Fuel Distribution

It is a kind of classic catch-22 situation with strategic paths and their impact on hydrogen fuel distribution. Once cars start getting sold with fuel cells they will need available fuel, and yet, if the adoption rate is low there won't be that many cars around with the need for hydrogen fuel. Over time, a complex and expensive logistical fuel distribution network must be set up, and the type of hydrogen fuel, again, will be contingent upon the specific technologies chosen on the strategic path for cars. Who will decide to invest in hydrogen fuel distribution? Whether it will be the traditional petroleum companies or other companies is one of many questions that are raised.

Hydrogen Fuel Stations

Similar to the existing network of gas stations, whatever hydrogen fuel is applicable for fuel filling will have to be available, again, whether it be hydrogen, methanol, methane, butane, or some other source. Will this role be fulfilled by traditional service stations as an additional fuel, as with diesel fuel, or will there be a separate distribution system? All kinds of other questions abound, depending on the technology choice of the fuel cells, regarding the type of fuel filling, the necessary safety requirements, and a whole host of others.

Fuel Cell Parts and Services

Part of the fuel cells market network will have to be the availability of parts and service to car buyers and car dealers for maintenance and servicing of the cars. Will this be done by the traditional car manufacturing service outlets who will decide to produce parts for fuel cell cars? Again, this is very much tied to the strategic paths that many other companies in the network have gone down and with which integrated.

Intranets and Internet

The role of the Internet and companies' specific intranets in this very complex fuel cell market network isn't clear. Many potential interfaces are possible in terms of the interchange of information and the communication of the strategic paths of other companies and members of the market network. It could be argued that the intranets and Internet will accelerate the integration of this fuel cells' market networks through their capacity to quickly move information and to reveal the strategic paths of other major players in the network.

Fuel Cells Market Networks: Strategic Paths As Cross-Company Linking Mechanisms

A simplified view of the market networks for the car application of fuel cells has been outlined. Clearly, even within this simple context the complexity of the strategic paths across the market network is enormous. The challenge it presents to every company in the market network is not only to develop their own strategic path that will produce high net cash flow for themselves, but to integrate, reconcile, and link their strategic paths to other critical companies with which they are connected in the market network. This is shown schematically in Figure 3.11.

The nature of these linking mechanisms, based on the four critical dimensions of each company's strategic paths, means that for any two companies, strategic paths can serve as vital and explicit strategic-linking mechanisms between the strategic-path choices managers have to make and those made by other companies. Four possible types of linkages exist that managers in these companies can utilize:

- Cross-company technology linkages
- Cross-company product functionality linkages
- Cross-company market network linkages
- Cross-company end-user segment linkages

An example of cross-company technology linkages is the relationship between fuel cell technology developers, such as Ballard, and the car manufacturers, such as General Motors and Ford. From a technology perspective, General Motors cannot put fuel cells into

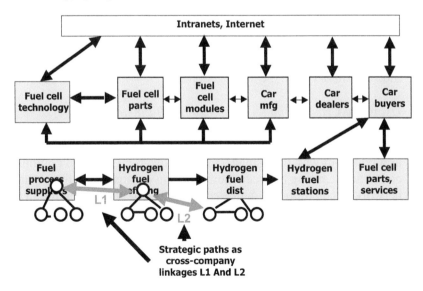

FIGURE 3.11. Fuel cells market networks: Strategic paths as cross-company linking mechanisms.

cars for which the technology doesn't exist. Their concept of technology and their strategic path has to be strategically linked to the concept of the fuel cell technology developments. One strategy for General Motors to do this is to become a technology developer and to have an intimate relationship with the technology dimension of fuel cell companies.

The same logic applies to cross-company product functionality links. Fuel cell technologies on the strategic path of technology companies, such as Ballard, may not provide the type of functionality that General Motors wants in its entry-level fuel cell cars, or may require extensive modifications. In addition to this, the functionality that is required of the fuel cell may change dramatically over the development cycle of fuel cell cars. Similarly, the nature of end-user segments, the people who are prepared to adopt fuel cell cars and continue buying them, may change over time, may dramatically alter the functionality requirements and, therefore, dramatically alter the technology requirements. All of these changes over time are reflected in changes in strategic paths of all the major participants.

The role of intranets and the Internet has been prominently featured. Much of the content of the linking of strategic paths is informational, and this is where intranets and the Internet come into powerful play. Looking at Internet sites for fuel cells, a wealth of information is available on the strategic paths being followed by numerous participants in the fuel cells' cars situations. This provides another linking mechanism between the strategic paths.

Using the Cross-Company Strategic Path Linkages

In this fuel cell application, using strategic path linkages can serve as a powerful way for managers to improve their focus of communication and learning between their different companies in their market network. It can motivate managers to study and understand the strategic path choices of other companies and more easily estimate their impact on their own strategic path choices. From a competitive point of view strategic path linkages can help managers to more clearly focus on their major competitors' strategic paths and to counter them.

Strategic paths can also be a powerful tool in creating and managing joint ventures with new technologies. It provides a simplifying framework to explore the primal elements of most joint ventures. In the joint venture, how will the different parties' involvements create cohesive and competitive strategic paths and net cash flow? Where will the strategic synergies be?

END-USER SEGMENTS COMPETITIVE SPACE: THE SEGMENTS BUNDLE

What do we mean by end-user segments? End-user segments are different bundles of end users for product functionalities based on differences in their choice, rejection, and usage behavior; product needs; and numerous other dimensions. Different bundles of end-user companies, buyers, and individuals who are impacted by the product must make choices between competitive product functionalities. The critical difference between segments is that they have behavioral choice, rejection, and usage processes around the product and technologies that are different from those of other segments making these choices. What is important is a deep analysis and understanding of their real and complex choice/rejection processes.

Also required when looking at end-user segments' competitive space is a deep understanding of the critical competitive product functionalities differentiation that will drive their choice. This differentiation will vary between segments. The critical thing is not just to describe segments but to create segments that you can competitively capture with a unique strategic path. In looking at end-user segments competitive space, a key analysis is to map all the possible end-user segments in a creative and analytical way.

Mapping the End-Users Segments Competitive Space

Of all the competitive spaces, mapping end-users competitive space is one of the most difficult. Much has been written about market segmentation and the basis for doing segmentation. The concept of strategic paths presents another useful way to explore different bases for end-user segmentation.

Strategic Paths As a Basis for Segmentation

Applying strategic paths, we can identify several additional bases for segmenting end-use customers:

- Segmentation by end-user company characteristics, such as industry, company size, location, global reach, need for product/services mix, buying style, central or localized buying, multisupplier usage, buying item by item or bundling, choice/ rejection criteria and process, and a host of company-specific criteria.
- At the level of car buyers as individual consumers and end users grows, a whole other range of potential segmentation bases come into play. Some examples are income, age, family life cycle, location, existing car use, purchase history, innovativeness, environmental concern, risk preference, experience, and many others. In the case of fuel cells, many of these segmentation factors will clearly affect consumers potential adoption of the technology and product functionality.
- Segmentation by technologies choice and application. Different end-user companies may have very different existing technologies bundles and infrastructure, which may impact their ability or desire to adopt a new strategic path.
- Segmentation by product functionalities. Different end users may have different existing experience with the complex sets of product functionalities, which will impact their perceptions of the differentiation of a new strategic path.
- Segmentation by market networks. Different end users may access very different and complex webs of market networks, using them for very different sets of services and support.

All of these can provide powerful potential bases for end-user segmentation in different competitive situations. The important thing for managers is to be conceptually creative and apply a number of these segmentation schemes to reveal as much as possible of the impact of different strategic-path choices.

An example of a map of the end-user segment competitive space is shown in Figure 3.12. Two key end-user segment dimensions are mapped to try to identify potential segment focus. The first is segment size potential. This requires making estimates of the relative

End-user segments

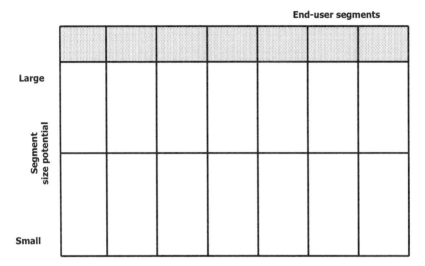

FIGURE 3.12. End-user segments' competitive space (S4).

cash flow potential of different end-user segments. To make these estimates, different bases for segmentation need to be developed that are unique to the competitive situation. The second dimension of this map is the end-user segments. You are seeking the highest potential end-user segments.

The Fuel Cells Example

Many diverse end-user segments are available for fuel cells. Fuel cells can power cars, buses, boats, trains, planes, scooters, even bicycles. There could be fuel cell–powered vending machines, vacuum cleaners, and highway road signs. Miniature fuel cells for cellular phones, laptop computers, and portable electronics are being explored. Hospitals, credit card centers, police stations, and banks are all looking at using fuel cells to provide power to their facilities. Wastewater treatment plants and landfills are exploring fuel cells to convert the methane gas they produce into electricity. The possibilities are endless. Some leading segments follow.

Stationary Power Segments

In hospitals, nursing homes, hotels, office buildings, schools, utility power plants, and airport terminals, fuel cells can provide primary power or backup. In large-scale building systems, fuel cells can reduce facility energy service costs to 20 to 40 percent less than conventional energy service.

Residential Power Segments

Fuel cells could be ideal for power generation, either connected to the electric grid to provide supplemental power and backup assurance for critical areas, or installed as a grid-independent generator for on-site service in areas that are inaccessible by power lines. Since fuel cells operate silently, they reduce noise pollution as well as air pollution and the waste heat from a fuel cell can be used to provide hot water or space heating for a home. Many of the prototypes being tested and demonstrated for residential use extract hydrogen from propane or natural gas.

Transportation Segments

All the major automotive manufacturers have a fuel cell vehicle either in development or in testing right now. Honda and Toyota have already begun testing vehicles in California and Japan. Automakers and some experts speculate that the fuel cell vehicle will not be commercialized until at least 2010. Fuel cells may also be incorporated into buses, locomotives, airplanes, scooters, and golf carts.

Portable Power Segments

Miniature fuel cells, once available to the commercial market, may help consumers talk for up to a month on a cellular phone without recharging. Fuel cells may change the telecommuting world, powering laptops and palm pilots hours longer than batteries. Other potential applications for micro fuel cells include pagers, video recorders, portable power tools, and low-power remote devices such as hearing aids, smoke detectors, burglar alarms, hotel locks, and meter readers. These miniature fuel cells generally run on methanol, an inexpensive wood alcohol also used in windshield wiper fluid.

Landfill/Wastewater Treatment Segments

Fuel cells could currently operate at landfills and wastewater treatment plants across the country, proving themselves as a valid technology for reducing emissions and generating power from the methane gas they produce.

WHY ARE THESE FOUR STRATEGIC CHOICES SO CRITICAL?

The power of strategic paths is to focus managers on four primal areas of strategic choice: choice of technologies bundle, product functionalities bundle, end-user segment bundle, and market network bundle. The importance of these four critical choices on the strategic path is summarized in the following sections:

They Are the Most Costly

In the case of new technologies development and application in the future, there is no doubt that, globally, the cash flow in investments and fixed costs will far exceed those spent on any other strategic element. Trillions of dollars are clearly involved globally. Similarly, the transformation of new technologies into actual products with differentiated functionality is extraordinarily costly. Determining end-user segments that will rapidly adopt the products developed is expensive. Creating and managing complex market networks will be very expensive. Taken together, these four strategic choices represent, by far, the most expensive elements of strategy for technology-intensive companies.

They Have Long-Lasting Impact

Each of the four strategic choices is difficult to change once fundamental decisions have been made. In technologies competitive space, it is frequently very difficult to make a significant change once you have made a choice regarding the complex technologies and the way they are bundled. The same is true with product functionalities. Once actually designed and in production, it can be very difficult to make significant changes. The same goes for the focused end-user competitive segments and the market and distribution and supply chains. Many of the other strategic choices, such as pricing, sales force deployment, and advertising, can be changed fairly rapidly, but not these four.

They Can Take a Long Time to Decide

Each of the four major competitive spaces that define strategic paths is frequently the result of months, even years, of anguished management decision making. They often happen earlier in the strategic planning process. A good example is technologies competitive space. The choice of the fundamental technologies bundle that goes into a new product frequently occurs early in the strategic planning process, even before much substance is given to the potential strategy.

They Drive and Constrain the Other
Strategic Choices

As will be outlined in the book, the sequence in which these strategic choices are made on the strategic path varies from situation to situation. Clearly, once the fundamental technologies bundle is chosen, that choice can drive and constrain all of the other strategic choices, including the choice of product functionalities, market networks, end-user segments, and a whole other range of strategic decisions.

This set of major strategic choices and their connections to strategic paths are shown in Figure 3.13. As shown, strategic paths represent the four most critical strategic marketing choices: the technologies bundle, product positioning (product functionalities) bundle, target end-user segments) bundle, and distribution and logistics (market networks) bundle. The other important choices are shown in Figure 3.13, along with their important interactions with other strategic choices, both on the company's supply side and their market side. The other important strategic marketing choices driven by strategic paths are those of pricing, sales management, and advertising and promotion.

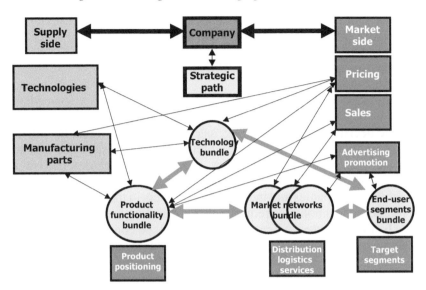

FIGURE 3.13. Strategic paths: Drivers of major strategic choices.

They Can Have Large Interactive Impact

When you look at the four major strategic path bundles, their interactions have been outlined as very complex and powerful, and potentially positive or negative. For example, a huge interaction clearly occurs between the choice of technologies and product functionalities. Similarly, a huge interaction occurs between what market networks are chosen and the end-use customer segments.

They Have the Greatest Impact on Success

Because of their other characteristics, as outlined, these four strategic-path choices have the greatest impact on success, measured as long-term net cash flow. This book will outline several examples of strategic paths involving different technologies, product functionalities, market networks, and end-user segments that doomed the strategic path to failure. In each case, each particular choice had a huge impact on failure, not just because of its nature, but because of its interactive effect on the other critical strategic choices.

They Can't Be Completely Controlled

In most cases, the four choices on a strategic path are somewhat, if not wholly, dependent on other companies' behavior. Unlike other strategic decisions, such as pricing, sales force management, advertising, and promotion, which can be largely unilaterally managed and controlled, the choice of technologies, product functionalities, market networks, and end users involves many other customers, suppliers, market network companies and individual consumers in the market. For example, some technologies require other supporting technologies in order to be implemented, which can't necessarily be controlled. A combination of the resources committed to these choices and the lack of control over them can make them extremely risky.

Companies Don't Have to Compete
in All Four Spaces

When you look at the strategic-path choices, companies can choose to compete and differentiate their strategic path in only one area; for example, they could license their technologies. Many examples of this exist. Companies can also compete strictly in product functionality development, and adopt technologies from other companies. They can choose to compete primarily in market network space. They can also choose to compete and access only end-user segments. Differentiation and competition can take place in any combination, and part of this is what makes the situation complex. Many different strategic paths can be pursued. This alone can make market focus a major challenge.

Each Area Evolves and Changes Differently

The rate of technological change and the evolution of new technologies can be quite different from the rate of product functionality change in competitive markets, the rate of market networks change, and the rate of evolution of end-customer segments. Each of these major decision areas can be badly out of phase with the others as they go through a variety of transformations. For these and many other reasons, the four primal choices on strategic paths deserve status as the primary competitive strategic choices that must be managed and integrated for new products and technologies.

CRITICAL QUESTIONS FOR MANAGERS

- Who in your organization looks at different strategic path bundles? Who is responsible for this activity?
- When you look at the technologies bundles in your products, which of these technologies have you adopted? Which have you developed? Are your managers good at distinguishing between the most important technologies and those that are merely necessary to make the product viable?
- Which managers in the organization make sure that all of the technologies choices for a particular product functionalities bundle are analyzed thoroughly?
- Are your managers good at recognizing the difference between technology in the truly physical sense and in the functionality differentiation? Do you have challenges in this area?
- How effective are your managers at conceptualizing and managing the market networks space? Is the use of distribution channels, intranets, the Internet, and various other network members brought together and integrated into one place under one set of managers?
- How effective are your managers at clearly recognizing and creating end-user segments in which you can create significant competitive differentiation?
- Of the four major areas of strategic choice—technologies, product functionalities, market networks, and end-user segments—in which are the most difficult for your managers to make?

Chapter 4

Managing Strategic-Path Transformation Processes: Creating Hot Zones

INTRODUCTION

The management significance and importance of strategic paths has been outlined with several examples. The example of fuel cells has been outlined in detail, to enable understanding of what strategic paths are, and of the inherent complexity and challenges of managing them well. For a strategic path, the four critical strategic choice areas of technologies, product functionalities, market networks, and end-user segments have been detailed. Managers faced with new strategic paths have to carefully make choices in each one of these four critical areas.

However, making clear choices of strategic bundles in each of the four critical areas is only the starting point for an integrated strategic path that has a chance of being rapidly adopted and creating high levels of net cash flow. The four critical choice areas have to be integrated; they have to support each other and be strategically consistent. We will now develop six critical transformational processes that represent the strategic connections that need to be made between each of the four major strategic-path choices to make them a cohesive strategy. The specific strategic-path example of fuel cells application to entry-level car power will be used in detail.

THE SIX CRITICAL TRANSFORMATION PROCESSES

As shown in Figure 4.1, six transformation processes strategically connect the four primal strategic path choices. These transformation processes occur from the natural interactions between any four strate-

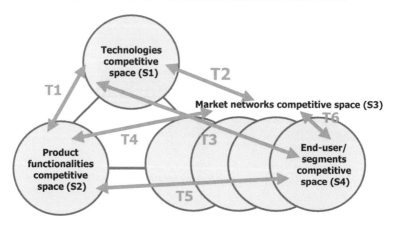

FIGURE 4.1. Strategic paths: The six critical transformation processes.

gic bundles. The challenge here is clear. For a particular strategic path, for managers to choose a strategic focus on bundles of technologies, functionalities, market networks, and end-user segments is one level of complexity and difficulty. Far more difficult, and much more complex, is for managers to strategically integrate these four bundles. A major objective of strategic paths is to break down the complexity and allow managers to deal with these critical strategic integration challenges.

Transformation processes encompass all of the management activities, analyses, and processes over the entire cycle of development and marketing of new technologies and products required to strategically integrate the four primal choices on a strategic path. By explicitly focusing their effort, analysis, and estimates on each of six individual transformation processes, managers can enhance the depth and quality of their planning. By looking at the six transformation processes together, managers can improve their strategic clarity and integration.

The Technologies→Product Functionalities Transformation Process (T1)

In managing the technologies→product functionalities transformation process, managers must strategically connect the bundle of technologies to the bundle of product functionalities. This transformation process must ensure that the best bundle of technologies and the best bundle of product functionalities mutually map onto each other, and that each synergistically transforms the other into greater market focus and competitive differentiation in the competitive situation. This transformation process alone presents many difficult challenges. For example, a new technology may produce an exciting physical phenomenon but no useful functionality for an end user. A particular technology in the bundle may constrain the functionality of other technologies. A particular technology may add huge functionality to the bundle but drive the variable costs out of control. One technology might be capable of creating differentiation, but cannot be technically bundled with other critical technologies.

The Technologies→Market Networks Transformation Process (T2)

Matching the choice of the complex bundles of technologies with the choice of market networks is an important transformation process. As individual choices, they represent great complexity. Each must be mutually consistent with the other and support each other. For example, a market network member may be unable to deal with the complexity of the technology in particular applications in terms of services required for the technologies. The market networks that are needed to work with the new technologies may have gaps. This transformation process is particularly difficult since it may be very different for different members of the market network. As an example, the complexity of the market networks for the fuel cells car application was outlined in Chapter 3.

The Technologies→End-User Segment Transformation Process (T3)

Matching the choice of bundles of technologies in the opportunity and the choice of end-user segments is a complex transformation process. It is especially difficult since a long and complex market network often separates the company's new products and technologies from their end-user customers. The bundle of technologies must be consistent with and supportive of the needs and perceived functionality differentiation of the end-user segments. For example, a particular technology choice may be incompatible with some of the end-user segment's existing technologies. Some of the technologies in the bundle may be too complex for them to use. They may not be able to backward integrate the new technologies into their existing systems.

The Product Functionalities→Market Networks Transformation Process (T4)

The bundle of product functionalities being considered must undergo a transformation process with the set of complex market networks to deliver the functionalities to end users. The product functionality differentiation must be managed so that all the market network members can actually understand, communicate, deliver, and service the functionality. Any of these members and many strategic areas can present serious challenges. The product may compete with some members high cash flow existing products. Some members may not see the product functionality as compatible with existing solutions they sell to customers in their network.

The Product Functionalities→End-User Segment Transformation Process (T5)

The bundle of product functionalities chosen must be transformed into focused differentiation that will drive buyer choice in the end-user segments. This is particularly important since end users represent the point of ultimate choice or rejection of product functionality. The transformation process here involves matching functionality to end users in such a way that differentiation and market focus are sustained and can produce high end-user adoption rates. Many potential challenges exist. For example, the differentiated functionality may be initially invisible to the end user until they have been trained on it in use. The functionality may not be easily compatible with end users existing solutions.

The Market Networks→End-User Segment Transformation Process (T6)

The market network choices and the end-user segment choices must undergo a transformational process that matches them carefully and ensures that the market networks and their complex logistical and informational interactions can effectively deliver the product functionality to the end-user segment. It is also important that market networks be consistent with the complexity of end users' choice/rejection processes. For example, the market network may not be able to connect to the end-user segment for critical services related to the product. The market network may not connect well with end users at all. They may not enthusiastically push the new product.

INTEGRATING THE STRATEGIC-PATH PROCESSES

As a result of the six transformation processes, a total of ten critical sets of complex strategic choices must be individually managed and integrated. These are shown in summary form in Figure 4.2. Four primal strategic path bundles are shown: technologies (S1), product functionalities (S2), market networks (S3), and end-user segments (S4). In addition, the six previously discussed transformation processes exist (T1-T6). Taken together, they represent a formidable challenge for managers. Decomposing the process and mapping them into organized sets makes the task much easier.

	Technologies space	Product functionalities space	Market networks space	End-user segment space
Technologies space	S1			
Product functionality space	T1	S2		
Market networks space	T2	T4	S3	
End-user segment space	T3	T5	T6	S4

FIGURE 4.2. The critical strategic path and transformation choice processes.

CREATING HOT ZONES

Six critical transformation processes have been outlined. Each of these transformation processes individually, and all of them collectively, are important in establishing strategic paths with high strategic focus and competitive differentiation. Not only must each of these transformation processes be managed well, but all six of them together must be integrated to create overall market focus and differentiation that drive adoption rate and net cash flow.

What Is a Hot Zone?

Strategic "hot zones" are shown simplistically in Figure 4.3. Each of the six transformation processes has been outlined as a process of mapping and mutually integrating bundles of the four critical strategic choices, for example, technologies, with another bundle of critical strategic choice, for example, product functionalities. The difficulty and complexity of choosing these individual strategic bundles has been outlined.

A hot zone represents the creation and management of three powerful strategic path forces: market focus, competitive differentiation, and strategic synergies. Each will be described in the following sections.

Creating Integrated Market Focus

In each one of the four critical strategic path bundles, market focus is the emphasis managers place on the most critical and competitively differentiated attributes of each of the four major bundles; where the focus is for technologies, where the focus is for product functionalities, where the focus is for end-user segments, and where the focus is for market networks. These decisions for market focus must be integrated; each strategic bundle must help to create focus in each of the others. Ideally, managers can create strong and mutual market focus in technologies, product functionalities, end-user segments, and market networks.

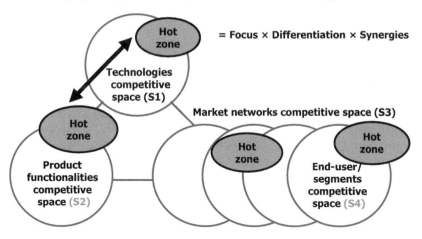

FIGURE 4.3. Strategic paths: Creating hot zones.

Creating Competitive Differentiation

The second major characteristic of a hot zone is the mutual creation of competitive differentiation. Managers must be highly focused on strategic choices in each of the four areas that create high competitive differentiation: technologies, product functionalities, market networks, and end-user segments. In an ideal situation, a strategy has high competitive differentiation in all four areas. Clearly, this is seldom the case.

Creating Strategic Synergies

The third critical characteristic of a hot zone is the creation, growth, and management of strategic synergies. Strategic synergies reflect the extent to which the focus and differentiation created in one bundle of strategic choice creates focus and differentiation in the others. For example, if the technologies bundle is highly focused and highly differentiated, it may create focus and differentiation for product functionalities as well, or for end-user segments or for market networks. These synergies are potentially very powerful.

To illustrate these concepts, a specific example is required. The application of fuel cells to cars is used here.

The Fuel Cells Example

Fuel cells' application to car power presents a set of unique potential strategic paths of great complexity and choice. This strategic example will be used to develop and explore transformation processes. As with many of the diverse potential fuel cell market applications, the potential global size of the car market is huge, as are the net cash flow potentials. Equally, the risks are huge. Already, some companies pursuing these strategic paths have had huge cash losses.

At least two major ways to apply fuel cell technologies in cars exist: fuel cells alone, and hybrid solutions with other power sources. It is important to note that these represent totally different strategic paths. When fuel cells are used alone, a different and more powerful fuel-cell system is needed than in a hybrid system. In addition, it is advantageous to use devices to store braking power for later use in acceleration. DaimlerChrysler's and Ford's prototypes use this method.

The other method is to use fuel cells in combination with batteries. In this case, the fuel cells act as battery chargers, while the batteries take the heavy loads and let the fuel cells operate more smoothly. Toyota's prototype car operates on this principle. Even though this is the most inexpensive solution today, it is by no means the only solution for the future. This solution also has a definite advantage: Most people drive less than nineteen miles a day, which is a distance batteries alone can cover. In this way, a car can be used as a regular electric car for everyday use, and only need be topped off with hydrogen when going on longer trips.

As a natural result of competition with fuel cell cars, more effective combustion engines, such as gasoline and diesel-powered engines will also be developed. Regardless of this, fuel cells may outperform some combustion engines because many people are moving to urban areas where traffic often goes slowly or at a standstill. When a fuel cell car stands still, just as an electric car, it does not use energy, and even at low speeds it is fuel efficient. A car with a combustion engine is most efficient at high speeds, but is extremely inefficient at low speeds. On average, a new medium-sized car with a combustion engine has a fuel efficiency of 12 percent. A typical fuel cell car with hydrogen may have a system efficiency of more than 40 percent, even at low speeds.

Fuel cells can also use hydrogen extracted chemically from natural gas, alcohols, naphtha (coal tar), and other hydrocarbons. This is normally done by a reformer between the fuel tank and the fuel cell that produces hydrogen-rich gas from the fuel that is then used in the fuel cell. Several car manufacturers seem to be opting to use methanol or gasoline as fuel for the fuel cells because of a lack of a hydrogen supply market network infrastructure. In the meantime, neither methanol nor gasoline will produce hydrogen without also producing emissions. The reformer will demand a lot of energy, require a long start-up time, and give poorer energy output than the use of pure hydrogen. In addition, methanol is also extremely poisonous.

This example of fuel cells for cars will be used to illustrate management of the six critical transformation processes as well.

MANAGING T1

Looking at the technologies competitive space, a huge range and complexity of potential bundles of individual fuel cell technologies exist in the product on which to focus. Similarly, looking at product functionalities competitive space, a similarly wide range of potential bundles of focused product functionality is available. What does the transformation process mean? It is the management process of transforming bundles of technologies into differentiated and powerful product functionality bundles. Managing it so that differentiated technology translates into differentiated functionality is critical.

It is critically important in the transformation process that product functionality differentiation be conceptualized and seen in the perception of specific end-user segments. The differentiation of product functionalities developed must be based on the perception of end users, not on the perception of the managers managing the technology.

Critical Management Questions for the T1
Transformation Process

- What are the critical fuel cells functionality needs for a specific car end-user segment? Before looking at transforming technology into functionality, it is critically important to understand the critical functionality differentiation.
- Have we mapped the product functionality differentiation from the car buyer's point of view along all the critical dimensions?

- Have we identified the highest potential fuel cell functionality differentiation that we can create from our technologies?
- Do we have the right bundles of existing and new technologies to create the critical fuel cells functionalities differentiation for the car segment?
- What would the ideal fuel cells functionalities look like?
- Have we created an ideal?
- How close can we get to the ideal car fuel cell functionality with our existing and potential technologies?
- What do we do if we don't have the ideal or best technologies? This is a critical question in the transformation process and may require the adoption and integration of other technologies.

Mapping the Technologies and Product Functionalities Bundles

The example of fuel cells for cars will be used to illustrate the importance of managers creating bundles of technologies and bundles of product functionalities that together can create part of a powerful, differentiated strategic path.

The Technologies Bundle

As shown in Figure 4.4, several critical characteristics outline the technologies bundle and some strategic possibilities for differentiation. These are intended to be illustrative only. Some of these could be the nature of the chemical reaction within the fuel cell: a reaction that is simple, with fewer parts, and that runs relatively cool in temperature because of the problems of safety. Reaction types that start fast, and are easy to refuel could be desirable. Also useful could be lightweight cells for manufacturing and assembly, a relatively small size, a high hydrogen conversion rate, and low manufacturing cost. These technical-performance characteristics would be tied to only a subset of the technologies that could be chosen to put together a fuel cell. They define a unique type of fuel cell that would likely be applicable only to entry-level, smaller, and lighter cars, and not to any other application.

The Product Functionalities Bundle

As shown in Figure 4.4, the product functionalities bundle has to be clearly integrated with the technologies bundle, and the objective

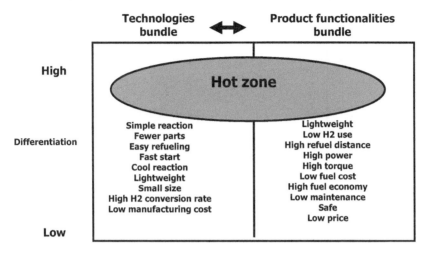

FIGURE 4.4. Mapping the technology and product functionality bundles: The auto application.

is to make them synergistic with each other. As shown, from the point of view of applying fuel cells to cars, characteristics such as lightweight, low hydrogen use, high refueling distance, high power, high torque, and low fuel costs define some examples of product functionalities that could create critical differentiation against other modes of power sources, such as internal combustion gasoline and diesel engines, hybrid power combinations such as gasoline-electric and diesel-electric, and others.

In looking at these characteristics of technologies and product functionalities, it is clear that companies in these competitive situations may have to do a great deal of research in both areas during the development of strategic paths. Doing the strategic-paths analysis can help greatly in defining these information needs.

Mapping the Transformation Processes: Creating Hot Zones

In Figure 4.5, managers can map technologies differentiation against product functionalities differentiation. As shown, when you map the two differentiated bundles together it becomes apparent at

Product functionalities differentiation

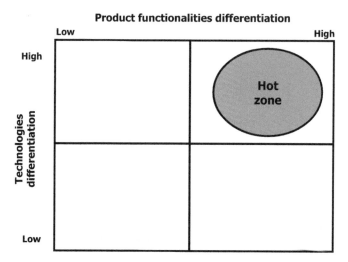

FIGURE 4.5. The technologies→product functionalities transformation process (T1).

which point the transformation process becomes critical. As shown, technologies differentiation for different individual technologies can range from none at all to very high. Similarly, product functionality differentiation for different performance attributes can run from low to very high. A hot zone is created in the transformation process when highly differentiated technology can be transformed into highly differentiated product functionality.

The more technologies and functionalities that can be mutually bundled into this hot zone, the more powerful the transformation process. An example of a "danger zone" in Figure 4.5 is a zone in which high technology differentiation does not produce significant product functionality differentiation. This is a frequent trap for technologies in which highly differentiated technology is seen as automatically conferring highly differentiated product functionality. Unfortunately, it is frequently not so.

MANAGING T2

Just as managers need to try to transform highly differentiated technologies into highly differentiated product functionality, it is critical for them to transform highly differentiated technologies into differentiation for members of the complex market networks that are crucial for delivering the product functionality to focused end-user segments. This is more difficult for market networks because there can be a significant number of members and complex relationships between them. This was outlined in detail in Figure 3.10. In this discussion, a total of at least twelve significant and different types of companies were identified for the fuel cells market networks. As a result, there will be, in reality, twelve transformation processes, each of which has to be planned and managed.

Critical Management Questions for the T2 Transformation Process

- What market network's infrastructure will be critical to support the car fuel cells technologies in use?
- Who are all the critical members and companies potentially in the network?
- Do we understand how each member of the network can create differentiation for the strategic path?
- Have we mapped the car market networks clearly in order to understand where the transformation processes have to take us?
- Will the car fuel cells technologies create competitive differentiation for key market network members serving the specific end-user segments?
- Can the market network members manage the car fuel cells technology complexity in use?
- Can market network members support the technologies complexity with services?
- Are the critical supporting technologies in place across the fuel cells market networks?

These transformation process questions are critically important, and in the case of fuel cells for cars, very complex.

Defining the Technologies and Market Networks Bundles

The use of fuel cells in entry level cars is being used as an example. Figure 4.6 illustrates some examples of characteristics of the technologies bundle that could create synergies and hot zones with the mar-

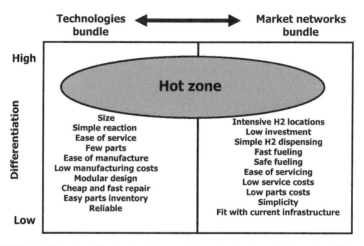

FIGURE 4.6. Mapping the technology and market networks bundles: The auto application.

ket networks bundle. Again, these characteristics are for illustrative purposes only.

The Technologies Bundle

As shown in Figure 4.6, in this case, some of the focal characteristics of the fuel cell technologies bundle may include simplicity of technology and reaction type, ease of service, as few parts as possible, moderate design so that repairs can be carried out without tearing the entire assembly down, cheap and fast repair, easy inventory of parts, and high operating reliability. Different reaction types, fuel sources, and technology bundles have very different operating characteristics, such as temperatures, pressures, fuel usage, service intervals, and many others. Another desirable characteristic may include smaller reactor size and weight. Many of these technological features represent trade offs, and these have to be made in the direction of creating synergies. In some cases, this may require applying lower-level technologies; the "latest and greatest" may not be the best choice in a particular competitive market segment.

The Market Networks Bundle

As shown in Figure 4.6, for the market networks bundle, looking at all of the network members together, some characteristics of the fuel cell technology may include the need for intensive hydrogen fuel locations, low investment on the part of members of the market networks logistical distribution channels, simple fuel dispensing logistics, fast fueling, safe fueling, ease of servicing, and low service costs. For the manufacturers of fuel cells, parts, and modules, low manufacturing costs may also be critical. It is easy to see, in this case, that the technologies bundle and market networks bundle must be managed together in an integrated and synergistic way.

Mapping the Transformation Processes

It is very important to map the new fuel cell technology differentiation against the network of market network members to understand where managers can create differentiation for different market network members. This map is shown in simple form in Figure 4.7.

MANAGING T3

The technologies→end-user transformation process involves creating a situation in which the fuel cell technologies can positively impact end-user (car buyer) competitive differentiation. In this case, managers have to transform highly differentiated car fuel cell tech-

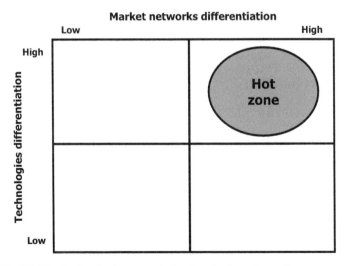

FIGURE 4.7. The technologies→market networks transformation process (T2).

nologies into highly differentiated end-user performance attributes. These attributes will have to be a strong part of end users rejecting cars with alternative internal combustion and mixed internal combustion/electrical technologies for fuel cell technology in the car they buy. This is likely to present a very tough challenge.

A complex set of fuel cell technology choices are bundled that must be integrated and reconciled with the complex functionality needs of specifically different car buying end-user segments. The differences in these car buyer end-user segments are profound. In this context, a number of critical questions emerge around the transformation process.

Critical Management Questions for the T3 Transformation Process

- How will different fuel cell technologies influence end-user car choice?
- What car buyer perceptions will form around different fuel cell technologies in terms of this end-user segment?
- Have we mapped the technologies against this end-user segment to understand the relationships between the two?
- How will end-user perceptions of the technology's complexity affect their choice/rejection behavior?
- How will end-user perceptions of the technologies bundle affect their expectations of after-sales service, vehicle reliability, and vehicle resale value?

Mapping the Technologies and End-User Segments Bundles

The Technologies Bundle

As shown in Figure 4.8, the fuel cells technologies bundle characteristics for the car buyer end-user segment outlined may include the attributes of a simple reactor design and a similarity in performance to the users existing internal combustion performance, including characteristics such as power delivery and torque. Simplicity of operation, equal performance to competitive mixed internal combustion electrical-powered power sources, low emissions levels, low fuel costs, and low repair costs may also be important differentiated perceptions for the end-user segment.

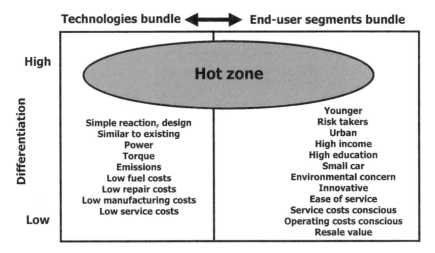

FIGURE 4.8. Mapping the technology and end-user segment bundles: The auto application.

The End-User Segment Bundle

As shown in Figure 4.8, desirable differentiation for the end-user segment may include characteristics of younger, risk-taking buyers in urban settings with higher incomes and education. Other characteristics may be environmental concerns, buyers who tend to be innovative, and buyers who are conscious of service and operating costs. Again, creating a hot zone between these two bundles is a question of making the focus and differentiation in both of the bundles line up together so that each reinforces, creates, and supports the other.

The previous segment outline is, of necessity, greatly simplified. Faced with this competitive situation, managers will have to carry out significant research to get a clearer idea of the critical differentiating technologies attributes.

Mapping the Transformational Process: Creating Hot Zones

Combining these dimensions is demonstrated in Figure 4.9, where the hot zone represents the integration of highly differentiated end-user segments and highly differentiated technologies in both of these bundles.

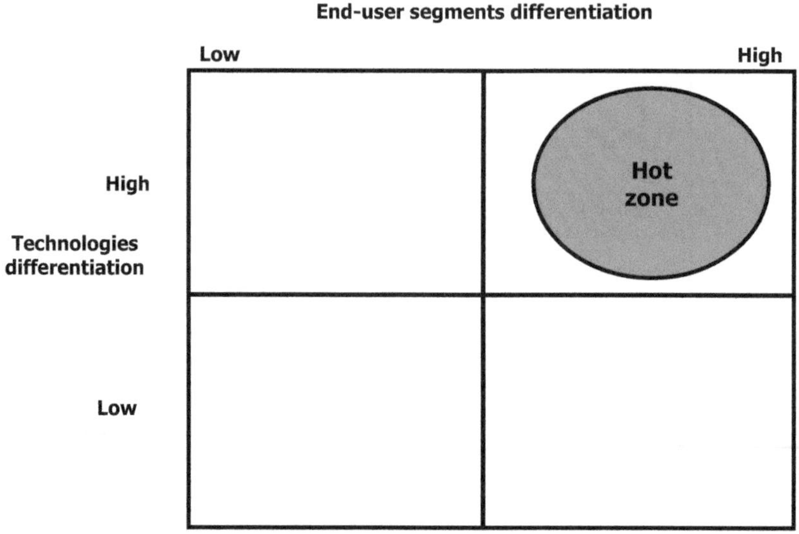

End-user segments differentiation

FIGURE 4.9. The technologies→end-user segments transformation process (T3).

MANAGING T4

In this case, the transformation process demands managers plan and create bundles of fuel cell product functionalities that create differentiation and synergies for different members of specific fuel cell market networks. Given the potential complexity of the market networks outlined, this can be a huge task. The functionalities bundle that will create differentiation may be very different for different members of the market network. This is outlined in detail in Figure 3.10. For each different company in the market network, there will likely be a very different impact of product functionality.

Critical Management Questions for the T4 Transformation Process

In looking at the T4 transformation process, the following critical questions arise:

- Is it clear what all of the critical fuel cell product functionalities are that will be delivered by the market networks for the car power application?
- Have the fuel cell market networks been clearly mapped so that the product functionalities impact on them can be managed?
- Have all the critical members of the market networks bundle been identified and mapped?
- Is it clear which members of the complex market network will be affected by different product functionalities?
- Is it clear what roles different members of the market networks will play in communicating, delivering, and supporting product functionalities to end users?

Mapping the Product Functionalities and Market Networks Bundles

The Product Functionalities Bundle

As shown in Figure 4.10, mapping the car fuel cell product functionalities and market network bundles, the product functionality bundle that will create differentiation for different members of the market networks may involve, for example, fuel cell reaction operation simplicity, low weight, reliability, low fuel use, few required parts and inventory, low service costs, low manufacturing costs, and a host of other factors. In addition, a major differentiator may be the operational similarity to current internal combustion power sources, from the perspective of some market network members.

The Market Networks Bundle

From the point of view of market networks, mapping the differentiating attributes that key members will want is critical. Looking at all of the members together, some important features could be the ease of fuel cell service, low investments necessary to get involved, and intensive geographic locations for fuel dispensing, sales, and service. Other important differentiators could be low parts-manufacturing costs, low operating costs, and ease of fuel manufacture and distribution. Clearly, focus in this area presents a major challenge for manag-

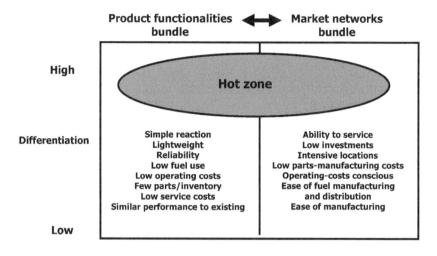

FIGURE 4.10. Mapping the product functionalities and market networks bundles: The auto application.

ers. As noted before, the analysis must be done for all members of the market network (see Figure 3.10).

Mapping the Transformation Processes: Creating Hot Zones

Figure 4.11 shows a map of fuel cell product functionalities differentiation against market networks differentiation. The hot zone identified in the map demands that managers combine the dimensions of product functionality that are highly differentiated and focused, that will produce synergies for key members in the market networks, and that will enable them to be highly differentiated and focused. Ideally, this analysis has to be done for each market network company, and then be fully integrated.

MANAGING T5

The product functionalities→end-user segments transformation process involves taking highly differentiated and focused bundles of fuel cell product functionalities and creating clear differentiation for

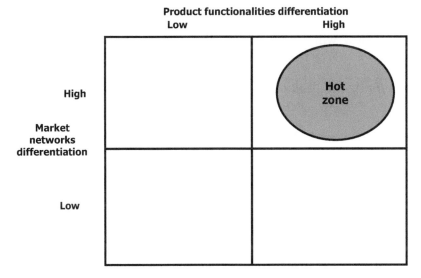

FIGURE 4.11. Functionalities→market networks transformation process (T4).

specific, focused, end-user car buyer segments. It also involves, in the other direction, looking at the choice/rejection process of end-user segments and trying to line up specific differentiated product functionalities.

Critical Management Questions for the T5 Transformation Process

Managers need to ask a number of critical questions when making this important transformation process:

- Is the product functionalities space for the car power application thoroughly mapped?
- Have the critical differentiated fuel cell functionalities been identified?
- Similarly, have the car end-user segments been thoroughly mapped so that all of the possibilities in the end-user segments are clear?
- Has the differentiation for particular end-user segments been clearly mapped onto the product functionalities competitive space?

- Is it clear that the fuel cell product functionalities can develop the critical differentiation the end-user segments require?
- How will car buyer's choice/rejection process be affected by their perception of fuel cells functionality?

Defining the Product Functionalities and End-User Segment Bundles

In the case of fuel cells for cars, the product functionalities and end-user segments need to be clearly defined. What is important to do now is to define the bundles in the two critical areas of the strategic path and to see if they can help create differentiation and focus for each other.

The Product Functionalities Bundle

The fuel cells product functionalities bundle is shown in Figure 4.12. For the end-user segments involved, some examples of critical product functionalities could be simple fuel cell reaction, low emissions, low weight, low fuel usage, low maintenance costs, high power, high torque, and operational characteristics similar to their existing internal combustion functionality. It is unlikely that any fuel

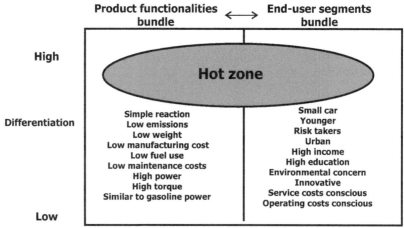

FIGURE 4.12. Mapping the product functionalities and end-user segments bundles: The auto application.

cell design can differentiate on all these dimensions. Again, the critical message is the need for focus on those functionality dimensions that can create synergies.

The End-User Segments Bundle

When you look at the end-user segments bundle, some of the critical characteristics for small, entry-level car buyers who would reject the existing product functionality for fuel cells may be younger buyers, urban risk takers with high incomes and educations, and with environmental concerns. They may also be innovative and sensitive to fuel cell operating and service costs.

Mapping the Transformational Process: Creating Hot Zones

It is critical to map the two bundles together. This is shown in Figure 4.13. As shown, product functionality differentiation is mapped against end-user segments differentiation. The hot zone combines the dimensions of each bundle that are highly focused, create high differ-

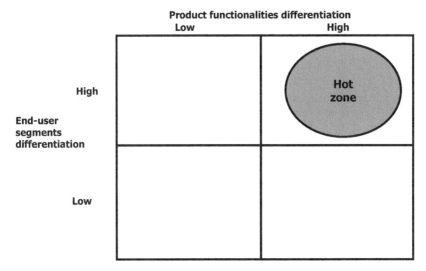

FIGURE 4.13. The product functionalities→end-user segments transformation process (T5).

entiation, and create synergies between the two areas for differentiation in this strategic path.

MANAGING T6

The T6 is the transformation process between the market chains competitive space and end-user segments competitive space. It is critically important to map these two spaces with each other in order to create synergies. In doing so, managers must ask several critical questions managers.

Critical Management Questions for the T6 Transformation Process

In exploring the fuel cell market networks→end-user segment transformation process, managers must address some of the following critical questions:

- Has the set of market networks that could serve the end-user segment been clearly identified?
- Have all of the market network members and all of the functions they must perform been clearly defined?
- Has the end-user segment been defined clearly so that the types of market network attributes they will need when choosing fuel cell–powered cars are clear?
- Has the capacity of the market networks to serve this market segment been compared to existing market networks?
- Is it clear that the end-user segment can be served by the specific market networks?
- Has the end-user choice/rejection/usage process for cars been mapped against the market networks to prevent any critical service gaps?

Mapping the Market Networks and End-User Segments Bundles

Again, the example of fuel cells for cars will be used as an example. The market networks and end-user segments for this particular opportunity are unique. The first step in looking at these is to clearly define the bundles involved.

The Market Networks Bundle

Characteristics of the required market networks bundle are shown in Figure 4.14. It is important to realize that the critical factors in the market network are those that the end users actually touch when they choose and operate a fuel cell car. Some of these critical attributes may be intensive fuel availability coverage of the market area, high service capacity and parts availability, and user-friendly logistical support. Another key differentiator may be the similarity of the buyer's car usage experience to their existing gasoline-powered usage experience.

The End-User Segment Bundles

The end-user segment in this particular opportunity is potential buyers of small cars who may have environmental concerns, who are innovative under the right circumstances, and who are very conscious of service costs and operating costs. Other possible segment bundle

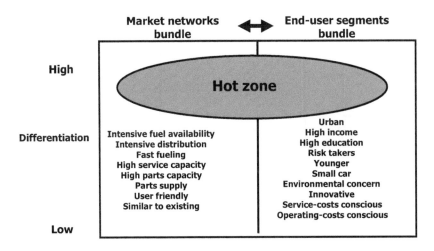

FIGURE 4.14. Mapping the market networks and end-user segments bundles: The auto application.

characteristics may be urban drivers with higher incomes, higher education levels, and of younger age.

Mapping the Transformation Process: Creating Hot Zones

Now that the two sets of bundles have been identified, they can be mapped together, as shown in Figure 4.15. The hot zone is a combination of high levels of differentiation in terms of end-user segments and the specific market networks who serve those segments. The combination of those two levels of differentiation creates the hot zone shown.

TRANSFORMATION PROCESSES AS STRATEGIC TRIGGERS

What Is a Strategic Trigger?

The four major choice bundles along a strategic path have been clearly outlined. The importance of integrating and transforming the

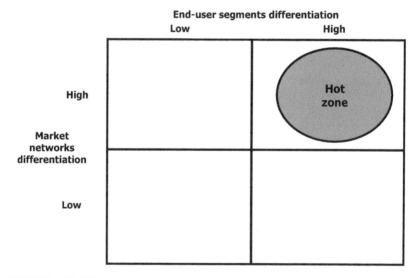

FIGURE 4.15. The market networks→end-user segments transformation process (T6).

bundles that these strategic choices represent has been outlined in detail. The reality of strategic paths is that the available choices do not very often occur simultaneously as we might like, but tend to occur, in many cases, sequentially. For example:

- In many cases, technologies become available and are developed that do some interesting, phenomenological things, but for which no current product functionalities are clearly defined.
- End-user market segments can have specific product functionality needs for which no current technologies bundle exists.
- Market networks can become available for which no current functionalities or technologies are available to fill the needs that the network requires.
- Product functionality needs can be articulated or can become available for which no technologies bundle exists, and, indeed, for which no network or end-user segment exists.

As a result, in many situations, a strategic path is initiated either with a new technology, new product functionality, a new end-user segment, or a new market network. The initial starting point of a strategic path is referred to as a *strategic trigger*. It is critically important to recognize when strategic triggers become available because they can become the basis for the development of the other three critical choices.

Managing Transformation Process Sequence

In reality, in most new product and technology competitive situations, the four critical choices rarely occur together. A large number of sequences exist in which they can occur. The critical question is in which sequence they are seen and managed by the company and managers involved. Four major sequences or patterns of transformation processes can occur:

- First is the technology-triggered transformation process, in which the company has some exciting technology that has no necessary, immediate functionality application, end-user segment, or market network to distribute to the end-user segment.
- Second is that a company will have some product functionality conceptualized or designed, but not yet a technology bundle that

will satisfy the design nor a clearly defined end-user segment or market network.

- Third is a situation in which a company may see a newly emerging market network, but no technology, product functionality, or end-user segment to bundle and coalesce the network around.
- Fourth, a company may have a clearly identified new end-user segment with new and unique needs but no current technology, product functionality, or market network to serve that segment.

Each of these transformation processes represents a different strategic trigger and different strategic challenges in terms of how managers organize to deal with and pursue these opportunities.

Technology-Triggered Transformation Processes

What is meant by technology-triggered transformation processes? An example is shown in Figure 4.16. As shown, the initial trigger for the process is in the identification by managers in the company of a technology component or bundle that seems to have unique differentiation and could potentially perform some interesting product functionality. As shown in Figure 4.16, in this case a unique possible set of strategic paths to follow. The technology trigger may lead down Path 1 to a search for product functionalities with which to bundle

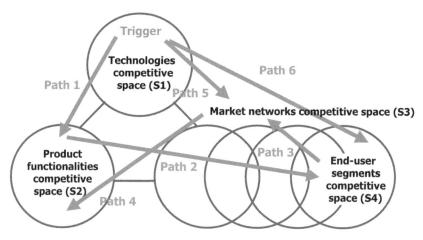

FIGURE 4.16. Transformation paths as strategic triggers: New technology-triggered paths.

them in such a way that they are consistent and integrated. This path, in turn, may lead to Path 2, which demands consideration of the end-user segment characteristics that will define the product functionality needs.

Exploring Path 2 may lead naturally to the exploration of Path 3, which is looking for market networks that are capable of supporting and delivering the product functionality to the end-user segment that is outlined. Path 3 can lead to Path 4, which raises all of the questions about whether the market networks can deliver, service, and deal with the product functionalities that have been bundled. This is followed by exploration of Paths 5 and 6, which look at the integration of technologies with market networks and the integration of the technologies with the end-user segments.

What we see here is not necessarily a desirable sequence of paths, but rather what happens when transformation paths are seen as the integrating mechanism that can lead to managers looking for the next path to go down in order to achieve the integration. This mechanism describes many technology-focused companies whose major competitive differentiation is based on "leapfrog" technologies. Ample evidence supports the notion that different companies will add the latest component technologies to their technologies bundle at different times and rates. In other words, they can choose whether or not to use a technology trigger for a particular product.

Some examples of companies who have tried to follow primarily technology-triggered transformation paths are Intel, Research in Motion, Vistakon, and Nortel.

Product-Functionality-Triggered Transformation Processes

In the case of product-functionality-triggered transformation processes, the impetus starts with the development or recognition or need for a product functionality bundle to establish differentiation. In this case, the first path followed might be the search for technologies to bundle together to produce the desired functionality. After that, a series of paths follow that are triggered by previous paths that might be very similar to the one exhibited in Figure 4.16. On the other hand, in different situations it might be very, very different.

An example of a functionality-triggered transformation process is the Biopure case, outlined in this book.

Market-Network-Triggered Transformation Processes

In the case of market-network-triggered transformation processes, a new market network possibility becomes available that opens up a set of new strategic paths for new technologies, product functionalities, and end-user segments. In the case of this new market network possibility, the first path pursued might be to identify end-user segments that can be served using the market network. After that, paths are triggered to technologies and product functionalities that could utilize the market network in accessing those segments. Again, we see different sequences of the strategic path being followed, depending on the triggers that are involved.

The best example of a market-network-triggered transformation process is the arrival and expansion of the Internet. The Internet has represented an incredible new set of market network possibilities involving new access to different types of end-user segments with different product functionalities. It has also allowed access to all kinds of other technologies, including software technologies. It is the best example seen recently.

End-User Segment–Triggered Transformation Processes

In the case of end-user segment–triggered transformation processes, we see the emergence of new end-user segments that were previously undefined and unavailable. Once companies have identified these new end-user segments this triggers paths toward new technologies, product functionalities, and market networks to access these segments. A good example of an end-user segment–triggered transformation process is users of portable telephones or wireless cellular phones. This segment, as a group of customers who have a whole bundle of other needs that could be satisfied while they are mobile and while they're using their cellular phones, could trigger strategic paths toward a whole host of other technologies and product functionalities.

The Importance of Recognizing the Strategic Triggers

Each of these different transformation process triggers requires a different reaction and a different recognition by companies. A company that relies primarily on technologies to trigger strategic paths has a very different style than companies who rely on leveraging market networks. It is very important for managers to recognize which strategic trigger they are taking advantage of so they can develop their maximum differentiation and core competencies around these areas.

CRITICAL QUESTIONS FOR MANAGERS

- How well does your company manage the technologies→product functionalities transformation process?
- How well do they transform distinctive competitive differentiation in technologies into differentiation in product functionalities and highly successful products?
- How well do your managers transform technologies into market networks competencies?
- How well do they manage the process of making sure that the choice of technologies is manageable and leads to differentiation for companies in the market network?
- How well do your managers connect the technological choices you make to the needs and differentiation creation for end-user customers of your product?
- How well do your managers transform product functionalities into differentiation and competency in the market networks?
- How well do your managers plan product functionalities to develop differentiation with the end user of the product?
- How well do your managers plan the series of market network members to develop differentiation and service toward end-user segments?
- How well do your managers tie all of these transformation processes together?
- What kinds of processes exist in your organization, including planning processes, to make sure these are explicitly and repeatedly done?

Chapter 5

Driving Fast Strategic-Path Adoption Through Market Networks

INTRODUCTION

In exploring the potential attractiveness of a particular strategic path, one of the most critical factors that will affect its net cash flow creation is its adoption rate. This is further complicated in many technology-intensive markets in which end-user adoption must be driven through extensive and complex market networks adoption, in which several different companies in the network must individually adopt and integrate the product. In the failure of many new products, a major causal factor is slow adoption somewhere in the market network. In a classic domino effect, failure to adopt at one point in the network can mean failure overall.

When trying to overcome slow adoption anywhere in the network, several key management questions arise. Mapping and understanding the market networks in which you will compete is critically important. Clinically mapping and understanding the choice/rejection process necessary for fast adoption for each customer company in that network is crucial. Another important area is positioning and differentiating competitively for every buyer interface to create buyer choice, and competitive rejection. Understanding choice/rejection behavior for every member in the market network is vitally important. Equally important is understanding their competitive strategic paths to see fit, strategic synergies, and competitive differentiation.

In reality, your managers may see other market network companies as part of your strategic path, but their managers see you as part of theirs. This is important to remember throughout your analysis and planning.

It is critical to note that fast adoption requires creation and brilliant management of the entire strategic path, not just the product functionality choices or market networks choices. In many cases, slow market and network adoption is the direct result of the bad technologies choices and the failure to integrate these technologies choices with the other key choices on the strategic path. In a very real sense, adoption of the entire strategic path has to happen for success.

THE CHALLENGE OF SLOW STRATEGIC-PATH ADOPTION

Managing the adoption of a competitive strategic path for a new technology has proven to be a complex and very difficult challenge for managers.

Creating Adoption by End-User Customers

In the real world, actual end-user adoption rates for new products are frequently far below managers' forecasts, estimates, and projections. The important aspect of analyzing and of managing buyer choice/rejection is to understand why many of these low adoption rates occur. The more realistic the end-user choice/rejection analysis, the better managers can predict realistic adoption rates and spot those strategic paths with little chance for adoption.

Creating Adoption Through Market Networks

In technology-intensive businesses, not only do new products have to be adopted by single customer companies, but frequently by complex networks of companies, both real and virtual. To the extent there is difficulty getting adoption by any single company, the combined effort of adoption down the entire market network can be frustrating.

THEORY AND REALITY

Strategic Paths: Forecast Adoption Rates versus Reality

As shown in Figure 5.1, a typical management forecast adoption curve, or sales forecast, for a strategic path frequently looks similar to a smooth exponential curve starting from new product introduction. In reality, this is seldom seen. More typical is the "reality" curve shown underneath. Frequently, significant lags occur between market introduction of a new product, adoption by different customers through the market networks, and a further lag occurs before positive net cash flow from sales of the product is seen. Many complex components of this lag exist, but typically they are not all accounted for in sales forecasts. These lags can have a huge impact on cash flow from the new strategic path, easily taking positive cash flow estimates to a cash loss reality.

In many cases, these adoption lags can be attributed to the impact of all four major strategic path choices—technologies, product functionalities, market networks, end-user segments—and their complex interactions. Some examples of potential causes of adoption lags can be seen in all four critical strategic path choice areas.

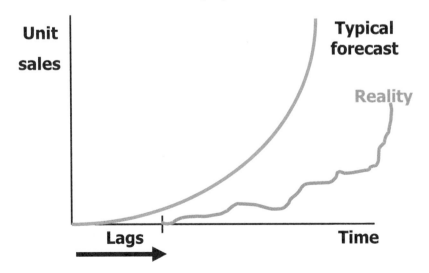

FIGURE 5.1. New strategic-path adoption rates.

Adoption Lags

End Users

- End-use customers have to reject their current functionality bundle, and they may want to get more useful life from it.
- Your technology bundle may not be compatible with end-user customers' existing solution bundle.
- Necessary changes must be made in the surrounding or enabling technologies for end users before your bundle can be adopted.
- End-user companies or other companies in the market network may have high inventories of their current solution bundle.
- Initially, end-use customers may simply not understand or believe your competitive differentiation.

Market Networks

- Necessary supporting market network companies or infrastructure may not yet be in place.
- The target end-user segment may not be currently accessible through the market networks.
- The new product may get stalled in adoption at one stage of the market network, sometimes for a long time period.
- No service capacity may be in place in the market network.

Technologies

- The technologies may be seen as not yet ready for application.
- Some of the critical enabling technologies may simply not be ready for application.
- The technologies may have some serious reliability problems.

Product Functionalities

- The product may not be seen as reliable and proven by end users or market network members for a significant time.
- The functionality differentiation may simply not be believed by some market network members for a long while.

For any or all of these reasons, a new strategic path may suffer serious lags in adoption at different stages of the market networks or by end users. The most dangerous result is often the devastating impact of these lags on net cash flow generation for the strategic path. In some cases, because of the peculiar cash flow dynamics involved, even a small adoption lag can turn potential success into disaster. These effects will be outlined in detail in Chapter 6.

MANAGING COMPLEX MARKET NETWORKS

For most technology-intensive businesses, companies are separated from end-user customers by significant networks of other companies. These networks are important on both the upstream-supplier side and the downstream-markets side. These companies include raw materials suppliers to end users and all network members from the real, physical, and logistical to the virtual, and all of their strategic interactions. Market networks represent a way of conceptualizing the strategic choices so they can be better managed. Depending on the situation, anywhere from a few companies and organizations to hundreds of different members can exist.

Successful adoption of new strategic paths is highly dependent on how well these networks are planned and managed, and how a strategic path will affect each member of the network.

Market Networks: A New Perspective

Market networks are a useful analytic concept that encapsulates and includes distribution channels, supply chains, value chains, the Internet, intranets, and all of their complex interactions. Some important characteristics of market networks are the following:

- Market networks are live, cash flow–driven bundles of companies and potential customers who must be actively managed over time as live members of a strategic path, not simply passive distribution outlets for new products.
- Market networks represent competitive, changing companies whose strategies and strategic paths may be driven by and consistent with yours, or not. They represent the need for continu-

ous change, the need to constantly alter strategies and company configurations within the network. They constantly mutate and change, and as a result the critical strategic paths change.

• Some of the companies in the market network may have much more competitive market power than you do, and may shape your strategy and strategic paths more than you shape theirs. They may be going down a totally different strategic path than you.

For example, Figure 5.2 shows a simplified example of a complex market network for semiconductor companies, such as Texas Instruments, National Semiconductor, and Motorola, competing for the antilock braking system (ABS) chipset functionality in the auto industry. As shown, a large number of companies in the market network all the way to end users (car buyers) of cars with ABS systems. This presents companies such as National Semiconductor with an enormous range of strategic-path choices with respect to how to manage and penetrate the market network. Their success, adoption, and cash flow in this business will be very dependent on the series of choices they make.

MAPPING MARKET NETWORKS

A crucial first step in exploring market network possibilities for rapid strategic path adoption is mapping the possibilities. As shown

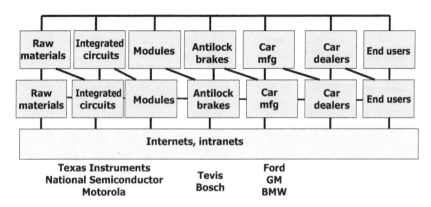

FIGURE 5.2. A simple market network. Cars: Antilock braking systems.

in Figure 5.2, five fundamental levels exist in the ABS market network: raw materials, integrated circuit suppliers, ABS module suppliers, tier one ABS system suppliers (such as Bosch and Tevis), and major car manufacturers (OEMs), including General Motors, Ford, Chrysler, Honda, Nissan, Toyota, and others.

In looking at this simplified market network map, clearly, an incredible number of alternative strategic paths through the network exist. Companies upstream, such as raw material suppliers and integrated circuit suppliers, such as National Semiconductor, will have many more strategic-path choices than will car manufacturers. The critical challenge is to plan a strategic path through these networks that will result in rapid adoption all the way downstream. This requires an intense and clinical understanding of the choice/rejection behavior of every customer company down the market network, and how they may react to a particular strategic path.

Choice of Market Networks

In the example shown in Figure 5.2, National Semiconductor and other integrated circuit suppliers are faced with a challenging set of strategic-path choices with respect to the market networks they choose to compete in. In exploring this it is useful to look at the market network starting with the end users.

- Car buyers go through a complex car and dealer choice/rejection process, and one of the criteria in this process may be the choice of ABS (antilock braking systems) braking.
- Car dealerships want ABS systems that will create car buyer choice of them and their cars and will result in enhanced sales and cash flow for the dealership.
- From National Semiconductor's point of view, in terms of getting their integrated circuits into cars, car buyers and car dealers probably have little power, initially. Their impact might be felt later, though, should reliability or performance become problems with the ABS systems.
- In the initial choice of supplier, the first significant company with power in the market network is the car manufacturer. They go through a complex choice/rejection process in choosing ABS systems suppliers.

- Tevis and Bosch are tier-one suppliers who supply ready-to-install ABS systems to the car manufacturers.
- Tier-two suppliers supply ABS modules to Tevis and Bosch; they provide pieces of the integrated ABS system that go into the car. Texas Instruments, National Semiconductor, and Motorola are tier-three suppliers who supply to tier-two suppliers.

Creating Competitively Differentiated Market Networks

Creating and sustaining the most competitive market networks for a particular strategic path requires active analysis and constant change. A set of key criteria identifies some characteristics of great market networks for a particular strategic path. In working with managers in this critical area, it is evident that the importance of these decisions is still not fully grasped, conceptualized, and managed in many companies.

Characteristics of Great Market Networks

For any strategic path, great market networks have some of the following characteristics:

- Strong competitive positioning and differentiation that is developed at every level and by every member of the market network. For each company in the network, significant factors provide competitive differentiation.
- A high positive impact on net cash flow creation for every company in the market network. This is developed in this book in Chapter 6.
- Strong relationships that are built and sustained with different companies in the market network that build net cash flow for all concerned and inhibit new entrants into the network.

These criteria represent characteristics of great market networks that must be continually created and managed. One of the challenges facing companies is adding more value to market networks to facilitate a more secure position within them. Changing the market network on the strategic path in terms of adding value will be referred to as *network rebundling.*

Creating Differentiated Market Networks: Rebundling

Market network rebundling refers to a strategy designed to significantly change your competitive power position and differentiation on a strategic path. The example of semiconductor manufacturers and the ABS system is a useful example. Three network rebundling strategies exist: vertical rebundling, horizontal rebundling, and mixed rebundling.

Vertical Rebundling: Changing the Technology/Functionality Bundle

As shown in Figure 5.3, vertical rebundling refers to moving the technology/functionality differentiation in the market network to the next customer, but not moving down the network in terms of dealing with companies closer to end users. In the case of ABS systems, an integrated circuit manufacturer can change the strategic path by creating differentiation in terms of integration or functions on the chip set, adding levels of functionality, simplifying the functionality, compressing the functionality (reducing its size), combining functions, or enhancing the performance of functionality. In this case, National

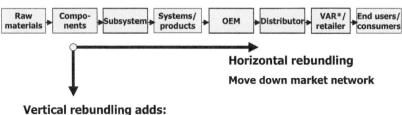

FIGURE 5.3. Strategic paths: Market network rebundling.

Semiconductor would still be a supplier to the module manufacturer and would not go further downstream in the market network, and could greatly add differentiation to the next stage of manufacturing. This strategy also clearly changes the entire strategic path for National Semiconductor in this competitive situation.

Horizontal Rebundling: Changing
the Network/Segments Bundle

As shown in Figure 5.3, horizontal rebundling strategies mean moving downstream in the market network so fewer companies exist between you and your end users. In the case of National Semiconductor it could mean selling integrated circuits in some form directly to Tevis and Bosch or even directly to Ford, GM, or other car manufacturers. Horizontal rebundling essentially takes the same level of technology/functionality on the strategic path and moves the company closer to end users.

Mixed Strategies: Combining Horizontal
and Vertical Rebundling

When companies get involved in network rebundling it is frequently a mixed strategy in the strategic path, involving a combination of adding technology or functionality to moving down the market network and changing their relationship to other companies in the network. Mixed strategies, or simultaneous horizontal and vertical rebundling, are what managers do in most situations (Figure 5.4). In the case of ABS systems, the mixed strategy might involve National Semiconductor getting into the module business and being a module supplier to Tevis and Bosch or even getting into the antilock braking business and being a direct supplier to Ford and General Motors.

Each of these three different market network rebundling strategies has different payoffs and risks and requires different marketing strategic skills and enhanced information.

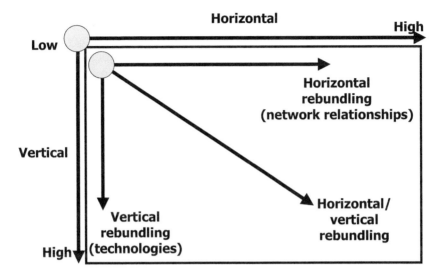

FIGURE 5.4. Market network rebundling options.

Critical Management Tasks in Market Network Rebundling

Vertical Rebundling

In a vertical rebundling opportunity, different strategic skills and responses will be needed, for example, in the case of National Semiconductor selling to an existing OEM that is producing components or boards. Such skills are:

- A capacity to enrich the OEM relationships. Given a much more complex technologies/functionalities bundle to manage and sell, a big increase in relationship people and time involvement will be necessary.
- Understanding the OEM cost base and cash flow dynamics. The major rationale for the OEM to want rebundling is to enhance its own cash flow dynamics. These can be very difficult to get information on, but it is critical.
- Understanding OEMs' customer segments downstream. The new strategic path will impact every company downstream of

the OEM. It is important to really understand all of these potential effects.

- Understanding OEMs' manufacturing technology and processes. The rebundling is likely to have major impacts on the OEM manufacturing processes, perhaps even replacing some of them. Again, the customer company has to see this rebundling as helping their cash flow.
- Understanding the impact of the rebundled technology/functionality through the OEM downstream market network. The change in the OEM-rebundled strategic path may dramatically change the entire market network which they reach through their customers.
- Large functionality differentiation advantage over OEM alternatives. The OEM will have other competitive companies to work with, some of whom may be offering more attractive rebundles.
- Clear understanding of OEMs' strategic path bundles. It is critical to understand the current OEM strategic path at a high level of management detail. In working with the OEM managers, it may help to try to get them to conceptualize their strategy in these terms.

Horizontal Rebundling

In a horizontal rebundling strategy, different changes are made on the strategic path. Different skills and responses will be needed. In the case of National Semiconductor, some of these skills are

- A capacity to enrich several relationships downstream in the market network. Moving beyond the existing OEMs that are downstream could mean working with a large number of customer companies with totally different strategic paths. Managing this is likely to require extensive and expensive relationships.
- Understanding the cash flow dynamics of all the other companies in the market network. A major change in the bundle could create large changes in some of their cash flow dynamics.
- Market-focused channel members downstream. If some of the other companies downstream have poor market focus, this could make the situation very difficult.

In all of these situations, it is critical to clinically analyze, understand, and attempt to manage the choice/rejection behavior of all companies downstream in the market network.

UNDERSTANDING COMPANY CHOICE/REJECTION BEHAVIOR

A Process Perspective

For companies in competitive market networks, every company downstream of them represents a potential buyer and customer. Each company has many choices of competitors and strategic paths to choose or reject. Each has many choices on which their own competitive strategic paths compete. The critical part of managing market networks is creating customer choice and avoiding customer rejection among targeted customers along the network. In many companies this requires managers to completely reconceptualize the way they look at their customers and process by which potential customers make choices and rejections.

A major problem facing managers in many companies has been focusing on product opportunities only in terms of competitive product functionality characteristics and differentiation rather than on the choice/rejection process that buyers go through over time. From a process perspective, managers need to clinically analyze the complex processes that customer organizations go through over time in dealing with new product and technology situations, and understand the conditions for competitive choice and rejection.

Analyzing and Managing Company Choice/Rejection Processes

Companies Bundle Strategic Paths: Customers Unbundle Solutions

For many managers faced with new technology and product functionality bundles, too much emphasis on analyzing buyer behavior is placed on looking only at creating customer choice. Faced with a potentially exciting new product and technology bundle, many managers behave as though their new strategic path is entering the market and end-user segment without replacing some other functionality bundle, and with no real competition.

The reality is that managers need to analyze both the choice and rejection behaviors of all significant members of their potential market network. Most potential customers in a market network have an existing solution bundle, no matter how inferior it may appear to your "solution." Therefore, most new strategic paths require buyers to reject some existing choice. Every customer choice has a component of rejection.

To explore these questions, we need to look at the choice/rejection process more closely.

MARKET NETWORK CUSTOMERS: FOUR GENERIC STAGES IN THE CHOICE/REJECTION PROCESS

Four broad, generic, temporal stages can be identified in any customer choice/rejection process for any new strategic path, as shown in Figure 5.5. A potential customer, at any point in time, can be in any one of these stages. One of the great challenges in getting new product adoption is in understanding when different end-user segments and market network members are in their product choice/rejection

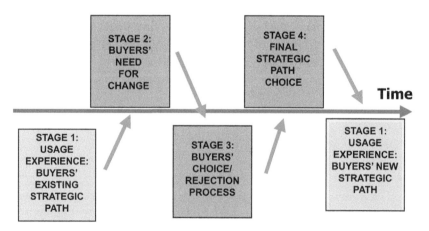

FIGURE 5.5. Basic buyer strategic-path choice/rejection/usage process.

process and how you can influence them to choose you, and reject the competition.

Stage 1: The Buyers' Current Strategic-Path Experience

Where in the product functionality usage cycle are different potential buyers in the segment? A significant number of potential buyers for a new product will be undergoing a current experience in terms of needed functionality from an existing strategic path. This experience may or may not be satisfactory, and it may have huge deficiencies. It represents the current behavior of the customer in the satisfaction of their functionality needs.

It is very important to recognize where customers currently are and to analyze exactly how your strategic path is positively differentiated from their current experience. Many examples of newly launched strategic paths exist that, although they offered great features and functionality, really were not significantly differentiated from the customers' previous choices.

Stage 2: The Buyers' Need for Change:
Rejection of Their Current Strategic Path

Buyers' rejection of their current strategic path is a critical stage in potential customers' choice/rejection behavior and is obviously necessary for the adoption of a new strategic path. Potential customers need to have a reason to reject their current strategic path before they can consider you as an alternative choice. Indeed, for many new paths, customer satisfaction is sufficiently high with the existing strategic paths that it may take a long time until they are ready to reject their current behaviour. In some situations, this can account for some of the significant lags in adoption.

Stage 3: The Buyers' Choice/Rejection Process:
Comparing Strategic Paths

Once customers have considered rejection of their current strategic path they can move into a choice/rejection process in which they look at competing strategic paths. In their complex choice/rejection process, for every available choice a number of rejections are likely to exist. An important factor in strategic path management is how to make sure you are not rejected by customers before they actually make a choice. The choice/rejection process itself can be very complex and can differ widely between buyers for the same path.

Stage 4: Making a Strategic-Path Choice

At the end of the choice/rejection process customers typically make a choice. They have made their rejections at some point in the process and are now prepared to stabilize their situation again around the new strategic path.

Stage 1: The Buyers' Return to Experience

Choice of a new strategic path leads customers back to the experience stage again, and likely to some reasonably stable period on the strategic path they have chosen, at least in the short run. Customers at different stages in the buyer choice/rejection process have very different sensitivity to new strategic paths. It is critical to understand where the segment of customers upon which you are focusing is along this spectrum. Some managers seem to assume that customers are always ready to reject their current path and make a rapid change. This is frequently not the case.

BUYER CHOICE/REJECTION:
THE CRITICAL QUESTIONS

A more detailed analysis of this four stage buyer choice/rejection process is shown in Figure 5.6. This process could be applied when looking at any specific new strategic path. The process is detailed in the form of five critical management questions (Q1-Q5). In asking these questions, you must compare your strategic path to the one the customer is currently on. This has to include your competitor's technologies bundle, product functionalities bundle, and market networks bundle. All of these are powerful sources of competitive differentiation.

As shown, most end-use customers have an existing functionality solution bundle in their current experience. At this initial stage there may be problems with them switching their choice. The first critical

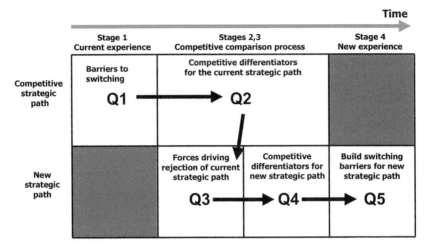

FIGURE 5.6. Mapping end-user segments' choice/rejection process.

question (Q1) is, "Are there any serious barriers to switching from their existing strategic path to yours?" These barriers may be related to the technologies, product functionalities, or market networks for the customer's existing solution bundle. In an extreme case, the barriers can prevent a potential end user from even considering your solution. Clearly identifying the customer's existing strategic path is very important.

The next critical question (Q2) is, "If there are no barriers to switching that cannot be overcome, what are the current competitor's major differentiators that captured the customer?" Do we clearly understand their current winning strategic path? This highlights the utility of well-understood strategic paths as a tool of competitive analysis. These competitive differentiators may be in the technologies, product functionalities, market networks, or in the strategic synergies the competitor established.

The next key question (Q3) asks, "What forces are driving the customers' rejection of their current strategic path?" What is their level of satisfaction? What is dysfunctional in their current bundles of technologies, market networks, and product functionalities? They may be looking at new strategic paths that have nothing to do with your competitive differentiation. For example, their costs may be causing them to be uncompetitive in their own strategic paths.

The next question (Q4) asks, "What are your major competitive differentiators for your new strategic path?" This brings into play your whole strategic-path analysis as outlined in the Management Application Toolkit. However, this analysis is only as powerful as your analysis of the strategic paths of your customer's existing strategic path. Your differentiation must be real when compared to both the customer's existing solution and any new competitive solutions.

The last question (Q5) asks "If you capture this customer with your new strategic path, can you erect strategic switching barriers that will slow or avoid your future rejection?" These switching barriers can be for any or all four critical strategic path areas, technologies, product functionalities, market networks, or choice of end-user segments.

KEY BUYER CHARACTERISTICS
IN CHOICE/REJECTION BEHAVIOR

It is important to clinically understand the details of the choice/rejection process of each potential customer on your new strategic path. Understanding and managing these characteristics should help managers create strategic paths that can develop powerful competitive differentiation in getting competitive choices rejected and in getting their product adopted.

A useful example here is the adoption of a new MRI (magnetic resonance imaging) medical imaging system by a large hospital. Hospitals are well known as one of the most complex and difficult organizations for which to seek adoption of a new strategic path. The new MRI technologies are very complex in design, operation, and service. The design and sales cycle can take years.

The Customer Buying Group

For any potential customer company in the market network, the buying group refers to the set of people in the organization who have some significant influence over the choices and rejections of different supplier strategic paths. This group is frequently informal, ad hoc, and often disorganized. It can also be difficult to see or access from an outsider's point of view, and may change dramatically over the choice/rejection process. It is critically important to understand as much as possible at the clinical level. A buying group is also a target for good market research. Several characteristics of the buying group are critically important:

- Different functional representation may be involved in the buying group, and this may shift dramatically as different considerations for the choice become evident. This is particularly important when the choice/rejection process takes a long period of time, such as for major capital products. It is critical to understand the membership of the buying group as it changes over time. In the case of the hospital example, a huge number of people are involved and interested, including physicians, radiological specialists, technicians, administrators, researchers, a whole host of committees (including finance and safety), and government and health care organizations, such as HMOs (Health Management Organizations). The concerns of all these people are as diverse as their membership.
- Every member of the buying group can play a very different role, either organizing, gatekeeping, being the "expert," or giving major functional input to the choice or rejection. It is important to understand how these roles develop as time goes on, and how they connect to the different strategic-path choices buyers have of technologies, functionalities, and market networks.
- Power will shift between members of the buying group as the choices and rejections proceed. Understanding where this power lies and how it is shared is critically important.
- Different members of the buying group may have very different criteria for success of whatever venture your strategic path is involved in. You may look better or worse depending on each member's criteria for success. Some may be concerned about the viability of the technologies. Others may be more concerned with whether the market network can provide good service. In the case of the hospital MRI, these concerns will, in many cases, be conflicting.

The most powerful way to become clinically aware and expert in managing the buying network is to establish powerful, long-term relationships with key adopting companies.

Buyers' Risks and Information Needs

Members of the buying group may perceive a variety of risks as the choice/rejection process proceeds and, therefore, need a variety of specific information to deal with the risks they perceive. Several aspects of this situation are important to understand.

- The nature of the risk is important to understand, whether it is related to the technologies performance risk of the specific strategic path, such as product reliability, safety, service, maintenance, or parts, or is a nonperformance risk involved with its impact on the adopting company's employees and managers after adoption.
- Understanding the kinds of information and their credible sources is very important. Again, building powerful relationships with buyers' organizations is the most effective way to deal with these challenges.

The Buyers' Internal Negotiation Process

The buyers' internal negotiation process deals with the complex substantive and political aspects of the organizational process that potential customers go through in the choice/rejection process. Involving different functional areas, hierarchical levels, and criteria for success, they can add a political dimension to the process that needs to be dealt with and thoroughly understood. The choice/rejection of a strategic path may, in some cases, have less to do with its excellence and differentiation and more to do with political process in the customer organization.

Again, the hospital MRI adoption is an excellent example. The internal negotiation process can be extremely long and complex. Radiologists can have strong preferences for systems that are seen as too expensive to the hospital administration. Equipment deals may have been struck across different hospitals in a chain. For these and many other reasons, selling into this process can be a nightmare.

The Buyers' Choice/Rejection Set

The choice/rejection set refers to the competitors' strategic paths in the choice/rejection process that are still viable choices in the buyer's perception, including the existing strategic path. It is dangerous to assume that because you are in the choice set at the beginning of the process you will stay there all the way to the end. It is very important to track not only your own membership in the choice set, but also your competitors' membership to understand the shifting criteria and nature of the choice/rejection process at any point in time. Again, the most powerful way of staying in touch with your position in the choice set is through managing intense relationships.

The Buyers' Comparative Process

It is important to understand, for your particular strategic path, how you will be compared not only to the existing path but to competitive path choices. Will the comparison be done sequentially or simultaneously? This involves getting in touch with the buying group and understanding all other clinical aspects of the choice/rejection process. In many cases, the comparative processes that actually takes place in large buying organizations can be very disorganized and chaotic.

The Buyers' Choice/Rejection Criteria

If you are currently in the choice set and are being compared to other competitive choices, an important question to ask is, "Compared on what criteria?" A simple answer seldom exists since the criteria can shift dramatically throughout the choice/rejection process, depending on membership of the buying group and other aspects of the process. Often, managers make simple assumptions about choice criteria when in fact it is very complex.

Clearly understanding, at a clinical level, all the characteristics of the choice/rejection process is critical to rapid adoption of a strategic path. In many cases, managers have only a surface understanding of many of these aspects and hope that the competitive differentiation they have created will result in rapid adoption. This is frequently not the case. A more aggressive attitude can be taken on adoption by creating buyer choice and a choice/rejection process in which you are the very clear and obvious first choice.

Again, in the hospital example, the real choice/rejection criteria may be obscured by the political realities inside the hospital.

CREATING BUYER CHOICE
AND COMPETITIVE REJECTION

The most important reason to thoroughly understand, clinically, all these aspects of buyer choice/rejection behavior is because all represent areas in which to create and build buyer choice while creating rejection of existing competitive choices. This has to translate to establishing strong positioning and competitive differentiation on the strategic path with each customer in the market network.

CREATING COMPETITIVE POSITIONING
FOR DIFFERENTIATION

Adoption of your new strategic path is clearly driven by the potential customer's choice and rejection process. In order to get your product functionality rapidly adopted, two things must happen:

- Some of your market network downstream members must reject their current strategic path and their current behavior.
- These buyers must then reject all competitive strategic-path choices except yours.

In order to make this happen quickly, and get rapid adoption, strong positioning and competitive differentiation must be established on the strategic path. Two critical dimensions of this positioning and differentiation exist. One is fit with buyer needs, and the other is differentiation against competitive choices.

Fit with Buyer Needs

A strong fit with buyer needs simply means that your strategic path is closely in line with, and fits all of the baseline needs of, the buying organization. This fit breaks down into two fundamental dimensions:

- The degree to which the strategic path fits buyer needs in terms of their direct use and solution
- The extent to which dealing with you, as an organization, fits the customer's whole choice/rejection experience over the whole product-usage cycle

Competitive Differentiation

Closely fitting buyer needs is critically important to be considered for the choice. The strongest basis for choice, however, is the extent to which your strategic path is differentiated against competitive choices. This differentiation can take place on several dimensions:

- Product functionality differentiation: the extent to which your product functionality is differentiated from existing solutions of the customer and against competitive choices.
- Differentiation of the customer choice/rejection/usage process compared to your strongest competition. As the customer goes through the whole process of relationship building and interaction with you, are there opportunities to create strong competitive differentiation?

FOUR COMPETITIVE ZONES FOR POSITIONING AND DIFFERENTIATION

It is a major challenge to get customers not only to choose your strategic path, but to reject their current behavior and competitive strategic paths. Figure 5.7 shows four strategic zones in which strategic positioning and differentiation can be created. It is unusual to find situations in which you can create positioning and differentiation in all four zones. In too many situations, little of the potential of these strategic positioning zones is utilized.

In terms of positioning, two critical areas are outlined: positioning against buyer needs and positioning against competitive choices. On the other dimension, product functionality and customers' choice/rejection processes are represented.

Zone 1: Satisfy Basic Buyer Functionality Needs

Zone 1 asks the question, "Does our strategic path satisfy the basic buyer functionality needs?" This zone focuses on developing positioning that will fit and satisfy the primal needs of the targeted segment of buyers. This is a crucial zone. In the hospital example, for which a competitive bid specification is likely issued, it means not being rejected on one of the bid spec criterion. It can easily happen that

	Buyer needs	Competitive choices
Product functionality	**Zone 1** Satisfy, fulfill basic buyer needs	**Zone 2** Create competitive differentiation on buyer critical choice/rejection criteria
Buyer choice/ rejection/ usage/ process	**Zone 3** Satisfy, fulfill basic process needs over time	**Zone 4** Create competitive differentiation of the process over time

FIGURE 5.7. Strategic paths: Positioning and differentiation zones.

you may have huge competitive differentiation on some more important criteria, but get rejected because of a missing basic spec item.

Zone 2: Differentiate the Strategic Path

Zone 2 asks the question, "Can we differentiate our strategic path from competitive choices in order to achieve competition rejection?" Zone 2 is a critical zone in competitive strategy. In many cases, positioning can satisfy Zone 1 requirements for buyer needs but not create differentiation to drive rejection of competitive choices. In the hospital case, this refers to the technologies/functionalities differentiation for the MRI system.

Zone 3: Satisfy Buyer Choice/Rejection Process

Zone 3 asks the questions, "Can our strategic path satisfy the entire temporal choice/rejection/usage process for customers?" and "Is everything about our path consistent with the entire process that customers want to go through?" In the hospital MRI example, this is a critical question. The system specification, choice/rejection process, and application of the MRI system is a complex cycle that lasts over many years. Companies such as General Electric are now competing more on a complete integrated product/service/relationship basis for competitive differentiation rather than just on equipment sale.

Zone 4: Differentiate Buyer Choice/Rejection/ Usage Process

Zone 4 is the most competitively powerful of the four zones and asks, "Can our strategic path differentiate the entire temporal process we take customers through compared to that of our competition?" and "Can we make the process easier, slicker, quicker, less costly, or more value-added in the eyes of customers?"

All four zones represent a range of creative alternatives for building customer choice and rejection of competitive choices. In every situation differences exist. Strategic paths can be much more powerful if all zones are utilized.

CREATING FAST ADOPTION

This chapter has outlined the concepts of market networks, buyer choice/rejection behavior, competitive positioning, and differentiation. Taken together, these concepts have the power to allow us to much more fully understand the behavior of customers and achieve faster adoption of new strategic paths.

Market Networks As a Series of Choice/Rejection Processes

It is important to look at a market network as customer companies who represent a series of complex choice/rejection processes. Every potential customer in the network can reject your strategic path. Clearly, all it takes to stop the network is one rejection from one key member. It is therefore critical to analyze and manage the choice/rejection process for every member of the market network, even if you don't have much influence over it.

Too many companies look at their customer as only the next member in the network and ignore the potential choice and rejection downstream of their immediate buyer. This can have devastating consequences in terms of total rejection of a strategic path.

In addition to every customer company in the market network representing a choice and rejection, constant change occurs in the market network itself. Members of the network can reject you at any point in time; you may fit the network today, but not tomorrow. Many strategic paths were securely located in market networks and then rejected because of dramatic changes in the network and in the competitive behavior of other companies.

CRITICAL QUESTIONS FOR MANAGERS

- Have you clearly mapped the alternative market networks on the strategic paths for your opportunity? As outlined, many potential market networks are available to take a particular new product to market. A specific path through these market chains must be identified even though it may change.
- Have you looked at each member of the market network as a separate customer? It is critically important to look at each company in the market network as a separate customer and carefully analyze the choice/rejection process and strategic leverage that the customer will experience as part of the adoption process.
- Have you analyzed the choice/rejection behavior of each key market network member? Critical questions to ask about each key member for a new product: What is their current choice for satisfying the product of service functionality? Why should they reject that current behavior and choice? How can you create competitive choice through differentiation of your product from competitors? How can you create strategic leverage? What impact is your product's functionality going to have on the customer's profitability?
- Have you anticipated barriers to rapid adoption by market chain members? It is critically important to identify barriers company by company, prioritize these barriers, and have clear strategic responses to overcome them.
- Are unit sales forecasts and adoption rates realistic? Do the sales forecasts for the adoption rates account for expected lags in adoption? Has the sensitivity of late adoption on profitability and cash flow been carefully analyzed? Is it clear to the management team what the minimum rate of adoption will be that will at least break even or sustain the opportunity?

Chapter 6

Strategic Paths:
Driving Net Cash Flow

INTRODUCTION

When exposing potential strategic paths to the critical questions, the most critical one to ask is, "Are we going to make money if we go down this path?" This chapter will reconceptualize, simplify, and explore the cash flow dynamic for a strategic path so managers can quickly and easily explore and estimate the critical components of net cash flow for different strategic paths.

The difficult management question of the validity of different measures of financial success for new technologies and products has been raised previously in this book. It should be a question for serious debate among professional managers in companies faced with alternative strategic-path opportunities.

It is vitally important to clearly connect the four different strategic choices on a strategic path to their impact on net cash flow, both independently and collectively. All of these choices, technologies, product functionalities, market networks, and end-user segments along with their interactions can profoundly impact net cash flow. For example, early overinvestment in the wrong technologies can require such a large initial investment, with the resultant negative cash flow, that no resulting strategic path can ever make positive net cash flow. Many examples of this exist.

CREATING NET CASH FLOW
WITH STRATEGIC PATHS

When exploring the financial performance and success of strategic paths, this book will use net cash flow (positive cash flow–negative cash flow) as the primary and overarching financial measure of success. This is consistent with a number of large corporations, notably General Electric, who have clearly embraced net cash flow as the major and superordinate measure and driver of financial performance and success at every competitive level of the company This is not to say that profitability, return on investment, and other measures of financial performance should not be looked at, but net cash flow is used as the major measure for this book. From a finance point of view, net cash flow clearly is the basis all of the other major financial performance measures.

THE OVERARCHING FINANCIAL OBJECTIVE

Net cash flow has been defined as the critical measure of success for strategic paths for many reasons:

- The major drivers of positive and negative cash flow for any strategic path can be fairly easily estimated and related to the specific path. Even if net cash flow cannot be estimated directly at the product level, the effect of the major drivers can be estimated and net cash flow can be estimated. It is important that these estimates be made as early as possible in the new technology and product development processes, and that they be continuously and iteratively updated very frequently as a project proceeds.
- Unlike profitability and return measures for strategic paths, net cash flow estimation does not require precise fixed costs, investment allocations, and complex financial algorithms. It demands only that the dedicated fixed costs and investments cash flows can be estimated for a strategic path.
- Unlike profitability and return measures, it is difficult to manipulate net cash flow to make a strategic path look more or less promising than it really is.

- It is easier to compare different or alternative strategic paths on simple net cash flow estimates. These estimates can be quickly revised, and should be so on a continuous basis.
- For purposes of managers conceptualizing different strategic paths, net cash flow estimation is relatively simple. Indeed, the cash flow management that people use in their personal household expense management is directly comparable to cash flow management in a strategic-path situation. Since it is easy to understand, it is easy for multifunctional team members in a company explore and compare strategic paths on their net cash flow potential.
- The conceptual foundation for net cash flow is simple, and estimates can be made by any manager. One of the problems in looking at financial performance has been its escalating complexity, and its "ownership" in many organizations by accounting and finance managers. As a result, the strategic part of strategic paths is often cleanly separated from its financial performance. Many of the financial models used by companies are far too complex, stretching into many pages of detailed analysis. In this book, we will use simple one-page worksheets to make fast estimates of the net cash flows for different strategic paths.

POSITIVE CASH FLOW DRIVERS

The basic drivers of strategic path positive cash flow are shown in Figure 6.1: the cash flow dynamic. For a new strategic path, positive cash flow is simply the current estimate of number of units of the product adopted multiplied by the dollar unit margin per product. As an alternative, positive cash flow can also be estimated by revenue dollars multiplied by percent margin.

NEGATIVE CASH FLOW DRIVERS

As shown in Figure 6.1, two familiar sets of negative cash flow drivers for a strategic path exist. The first set is the estimates of series of fixed costs, which should be unique to the particular strategic path. The second is investment cash flows, which can be estimated and ex-

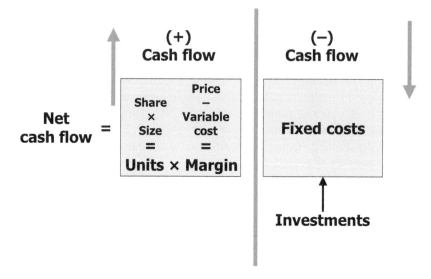

FIGURE 6.1. The strategic path cash flow dynamic.

pressed as the negative cash flows required to amortize the investment (analogous to a personal mortgage or car lease payment).

For a specific strategic path, the conceptual objective is clear: to build the forces of positive cash flow to overcome the forces of negative cash flow. In looking at this analytically, a useful tool is a profile of the estimation and use of net cash flow. The components of this profile are shown in Figure 6.2.

EVALUATING A STRATEGIC PATH:
NET CASH FLOW PROFILES

Figure 6.3 shows two examples of net cash flow profile estimates for a strategic path: a great net cash flow profile and a poor profile. As with most new strategic paths, an initial period of negative net cash flow often occurs during early product introduction, followed, hopefully, by a period of high and growing positive net cash flow. This is illustrated in the "great" profile in which the major cash flow drivers produce a relatively short and shallow negative net cash flow period followed by a long and very positive cash flow period. In the "poor"

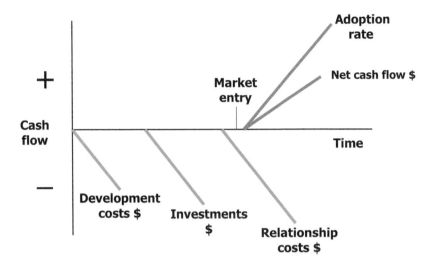

FIGURE 6.2. New strategic paths cash flows.

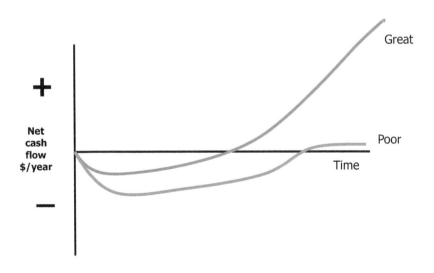

FIGURE 6.3. New strategic paths: Net cash flow profiles.

profile shown, negative cash flow is significant and for an extended period of time, and positive cash flow occurs later and is poor.

Figure 6.3 shows estimates of net cash profile characteristics, in terms of the magnitude and timing of the negative and positive cash flows for a strategic path. As shown, the worst situations are those in which the negative net cash flow is very high for a long period of time and the positive net cash flow is very low for a short period of time. Similarly, the best situations are the reverse of this. Looking at these cash flow profile characteristics, tracking them over the life of a strategic path, and constantly testing their relative sensitivity is critical to strategic-path management.

THE CASH FLOW DYNAMIC

The cash flow dynamic was shown in Figure 6.1. Eight major drivers of net cash flows exist for a strategic path. The terms in the cash flow dynamic are operationally defined and estimated as follows:

1. Market share (percent of units). Unit product sales as a percentage of the market segments attacked. These estimates must be corrected for market network access, and for the specific segment that the product actually competes for and has access to.
2. Market size (units/year). Unit size estimate for the accessed market segment.
3. Unit sales (units/year). Unit sales estimate for the product.
4. Price ($/unit). Unit price estimate for the product at factory.
5. Variable cost ($/unit). Unit variable cost estimate for the product.
6. Unit margin ($/unit). Unit margin estimate (price-variable cost).
7. Positive cash flow ($/year). Positive cash flow estimate (unit sales × unit margin).
8. Negative cash flow ($/year). All estimated fixed costs estimates dedicated to the product, free of allocations. These should include imputed investment costs (interest, cost of capital).

This simple cash flow dynamic should focus on fast estimates of net cash flow over the estimated life of a strategic path. Discounting these cash flows to a return measure is common financial methodology, and can be done for longer time-horizon situations. The nature of the cash flow drivers can change dramatically over time, with huge impacts on cash flow. Understanding the cash flow dynamic more clearly lets managers predict more accurately where major gains and losses in cash flow can be made with changes to the strategic path. It can also promote sensitivity analysis to find which of the four major strategic choices has the greatest potential impact on net cash flow over time.

The major cash flow drivers are well defined conceptually and operationally, yet, frequently, ambiguity exists in management practice about what some of them mean.

- Market share estimates should preferably be in unit terms rather than dollar terms, and should be a share of accessed segment rather than a share of overall market to avoid the trap of appearing to have a very small market share but having a very high share in certain focused segments. This is particularly important because a critical part of the strategic path is clearly identifying the end-user segments on which you want to focus the strategy.
- A particularly important cash flow driver is unit variable cost. It is critically important that these costs be truly variable and do not include allocation of investments and fixed costs. This is a continuing problem for many managers.
- Fixed costs in the strategic path are conceptually clear but have been troublesome for many companies. These cost estimates should ideally include only those incremental fixed costs that are specific to the strategic path, and not those allocated from other sources. The same is true of investments.

For many strategic paths over their development cycle, different quality of information is available on the eight major cash flow drivers. It is important when exploring a strategic path to identify those that have the greatest uncertainty and the poorest information and to try to significantly upgrade them.

AN IDEAL SCENARIO

In looking at the major drivers in the cash flow dynamic, an ideal strategic path scenario emerges. This is unlikely to be seen in many competitive situations, but is a useful comparison for any strategic path to identify the factors that will drive cash flow in the situation.

An ideal strategic path has the following characteristics:

- A large and growing end-user segment
- High market share potential and rapid adoption rate
- High and stable price points
- Low and reducible variable costs
- High and stable unit margins
- Low and controllable fixed costs
- Low and controllable investments

The key here is to look carefully at the impact of poor performance in any one of these areas, and its potential impact on net cash flow.

THE CRITICAL ROLE OF PRICING

In looking at the cash flow dynamic, it is clear that pricing can play a critical role for new strategic paths, both on market entry and as the life cycle moves on. Conceptualizing new technologies and products as strategic paths changes the way managers have to conceptualize, plan, and manage potential pricing strategies.

Strategic Paths and Pricing

One of the most difficult decisions managers have to make for new technologies and products is not only initial pricing points but pricing on several different interfaces within the market networks. If a complex market network is involved, a whole series of prices is involved. The competitive situation becomes even more complex if the technology is embodied in a product that is part of someone else's product bundle, such as a component in a laptop or a fuel cell, for example. Pricing becomes a very difficult strategic decision to make.

The concept of strategic paths urges managers to think about integrating the four major strategic choices and bundles as early as possible in the technology and product development process. Along with this goes the consideration of costs and pricing. The great danger here is that if pricing is not considered early enough, the price of a component or product into the market network and into the end-user application may be significantly higher than the value and competitive differentiation it presents. This can result in product failure that seems to be a pricing failure, but is, in fact, the failure of a strategic path.

An enormous amount has been written in the literature about pricing strategy. This book will not report and condense all of this, but rather highlight some of the special conditions for pricing that are brought about by conceptualizing new products and technologies as strategic paths. This generates a whole new additional set of critical pricing questions that concern managers as they move toward a strategic path.

Pricing and the Cash Flow Dynamic

Pricing for a strategic path is connected, clearly, to the cash flow dynamic, as shown in Figure 6.4. Pricing decisions have impact across a strategic path but, most important, with respect to price, variable cost, and unit margin, they have impact on the product or the component. As shown, the most direct impact of prices is on the critical decisions.

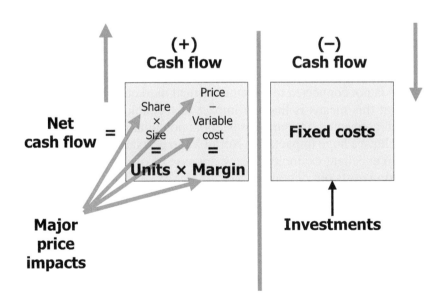

FIGURE 6.4. Pricing: Impact on the cash flow dynamic.

For example, if the strategic path involves significantly higher negative cash flow (in terms of fixed costs and investments) than were anticipated, a desperate need for positive cash flow is created on the other side of the cash flow dynamic. For most new products, the easiest response to a greater need for cash flow is to think about increasing price. The cash flow dynamic shown in Figure 6.4 effectively connects price to many other major factors that impact on the cash flow from a strategic path.

With respect to variable costs, a connection clearly exists between the technology choices on the strategic path and the variable cost of producing and networking the product. This will be discussed in detail in the next section.

Looking at the cash flow dynamic in Figure 6.4 it becomes clear that each of the four major strategic choices bundles on the strategic path can have an enormous impact on this cash flow dynamic. Each of these choices will now be discussed in turn. What it means is that, for all of the choices on a strategic path, the impact the choices will have on negative cash flow and on variable costs needs to be tracked very closely over time and their impact on price continuously estimated and reestimated before market entry.

The Impact of Technology Choices

As outlined in this book, all too frequently the choice of technologies is not connected to the other critical marketing strategy choices. What this means is that the impact of technologies choice has not been connected, in many cases, to its potential impact on pricing. It can have a huge impact. The Nortel Vantage example outlined earlier is an excellent example. This was a case of overexotic technologies driving costs out of control.

Technology differentiation is important to pricing. The more highly the technology is differentiated and this differentiation translates into product functionality differentiation the more potential value is delivered to end-use customers and, therefore, the higher the pricing that might be contemplated. If the technologies bundle creates synergies with other technologies it may have a highly positive impact on the perceived cost and value to end users and may, again, allow higher pricing. The cost of developing and manufacturing the individual technology as well as the bundle of technologies has a very influential impact on pricing.

Figure 6.5 shows an example of the impact of technologies choice on pricing. As shown, a situation in which the technology transforms into high functionality differentiation with relatively low cost to bundle the technology represents a best-case situation in its impact on the possibility of pricing and margin creation. Also shown in Figure 6.5 is a worst case scenario in which the technology doesn't translate clearly into much functionality differentiation and the costs of bundling the technology are high. In this case, the high cost of bundling will tend to lead to higher price that is not connected to greater functionality differentiation, which is not competitively useful. All of these connections between the technologies bundle and pricing must be carefully considered by managers.

The Impact of Product Functionality Choices

Product functionality is what the end users and market network members see and make choices and rejections on. In the case of a technology for which the end user may not make choices, the primary

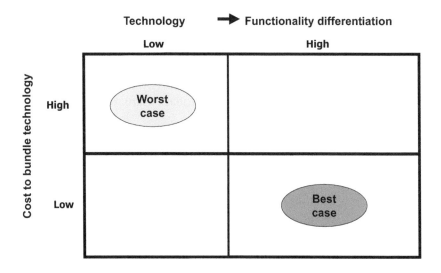

FIGURE 6.5. Impact of technologies choice on pricing: Costs to bundle versus differentiation.

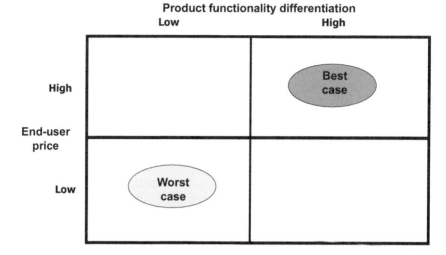

FIGURE 6.6. Pricing: Price and product functionality differentiation.

connection with price is through costs. In the case of product functionality, the primary connection is through differentiation and price. Higher product functionality differentiation that is useful to end users will support higher prices on product introduction. This is shown schematically in Figure 6.6, in which for the best case scenario, high product functionality differentiation can support a high price, and the worst case scenario, low product functionality differentiation, will tend to be consistent with a lower price. Other major factors that come into play with product functionality are the product functionalities bundle synergies.

The extent that functionalities synergistically present more differentiation for customers can support a higher price. Other major factors that can connect product functionality choices and price are as follows:

- The clarity of current competitive product functionality. If it is clear to the customers that the functionality differentiation is being replaced because the current functionality is clearer, a higher price can be favorably supported.
- If the technology fits with the customer's current infrastructure around the functionality bundle

- If the product manufacturing costs and product service costs are manageable
- If the product life-cycle costs are manageable by the customer
- If the functionalities bundle is not too complex to be understood

All of these factors can influence price based on product functionality choices.

The Impact of End-User Segment Choices

Here we are talking about factors that impact price based on the end-user target segments to which the strategic path directs itself. Some of the factors that have a strong influence on price are:

- The size of the segment and its growth rate. Much larger segments with a much higher growth rate present much more flexibility and opportunity for a pricing strategy than small segments that are not growing quickly.
- The ease of the customers understanding the product functionalities differentiation. End-user segments clearly understanding and seeing the differentiation is a good sign for an aggressive pricing strategy.
- The ease with which buyers can go through the choice/rejection process for the new strategic path.
- The ease of competitive comparison and clarity of current buyer choices. The extent to which this satisfaction can be more seriously seen, with respect to the existing solution compared to the new strategic path, allows much more flexibility in pricing.
- The ability of the potential buyer to reject the current functionality and their capacity to retrofit or integrate the new strategic path functionality with their existing solution.
- The impact on the end-user's cash flow dynamics and competitive prices.

Another important factor is price sensitivity. As shown in Figure 6.7, if the end user has very high price sensitivity, it will be easier to move in with a low price, whereas if the end user has very low price sensitivity, it will be easier to move in with a high price.

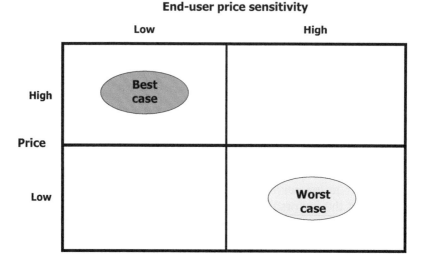

FIGURE 6.7. Pricing: Impact of buyer price sensitivity.

Similarly, price and adoption rates by end users can be related. As shown in Figure 6.8, end-user adoption rate of higher prices will tend to be lower and at lower prices will tend to be higher. However, these adoption rates have to be coupled with the other information in the cash flow dynamic to relate adoption rate to net cash flow development.

The Impact of Market Network Choices

A number of significant factors connect market network choice to pricing. None of these factors are simple. These factors are discussed further later in the chapter. The degree to which market networks are differentiated from existing market networks can have an impact on pricing. The market network synergies and the impact to which they have synergies among the network can offer much greater opportunity for aggressive pricing. In addition, market network strategic leverage is very important and is discussed in a separate section in this chapter. The fit with the existing market network is important. If the fit with the existing market network is large, then less margin demands will occur in the network. The extent of market network sell-

End-user adoption rate

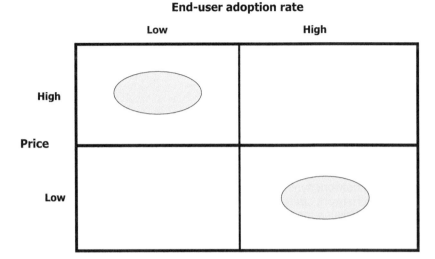

FIGURE 6.8. Pricing: Price and adoption rate.

ing and support costs can be very important. If these costs are higher, then more aggressive pricing may be required to cover them. The market network's life-cycle costs are critically influential on the extent to which market networks costs are high, and parts and service over the life cycle of the strategic path pricing will have to take this into consideration. The requirement for margins in market networks will be very critical. This, again, goes back to a strategic leverage analysis. Strategic leverage looks carefully at the cash flow dynamic and network price sensitivity. These major impacts between the strategic paths and pricing are summarized in Exhibit 6.1.

CALCULATING KEY SENSITIVITIES IN POSITIVE CASH FLOW

In managing a strategic path over time, much emphasis should be given to exploring changes in strategic paths in which the greatest gains in positive cash flow can be made. A tool that can help this analysis is the positive cash flow (unit/margin) map shown in Figure 6.9. This map allows different strategic path opportunities to be mapped

EXHIBIT 6.1. Strategic paths and pricing: major management factors.

Technologies choices

Technologies differentiation
Technologies bundle synergies
Individual technologies costs
Technologies bundle costs
Complexity of technologies bundle

Market network choices

Market networks differentiation
Market network synergies
Market network strategic leverage
Fit with existing market network
Market networks selling and support costs
Market networks life-cycle costs
Market network margins
Market networks cash flow dynamics
Market networks price sensitivity

Product functionalities choices

Product functionalities differentiation
Product functionalities bundle synergies
Clarity of current competitive product functionality
Fit with current infrastructure
Product manufacturing costs
Product service costs
Product life-cycle costs
Complexity of functionalities bundle

End-user segments choices

Segment size
Segment growth rate
Ease of understanding product functionalities
    differentiation
Ease of buyer choice/rejection process
Ease of competitive comparison
Clarity of current buyer choices
Ability of buyer to reject current functionality
Ability to retrofit or integrate functionality
Impact on end-user cash flow dynamics
Competitive prices
End-user price sensitivity

on the basis of their unit sales, unit margin, and, therefore, positive cash flow creation. Looking at the map, the best situation for any strategic path is high unit sales and high unit dollar margin, which means high positive cash flow creation. Given a strategic path with high positive cash flow, negative cash flows will have to be very high as well as for net cash flow to not occur.

Strategic Path Danger Zones

Figure 6.9 produces a concept of two danger zones for strategic paths: the low margin danger zone and the low unit danger zone. These are danger zones because minor changes can lead to huge declines in net positive cash flow.

The Low Margin Danger Zone

Strategic paths in this danger zone have relatively high unit sales but very low dollar unit margins. As a result, a small drop in unit margin can have a devastating effect on positive cash flow. Strategies for creating and managing strategic paths in the low margin danger zone are somewhat different. Looking at the cash flow dynamic, major focus in the process should be on managing price and variable costs for

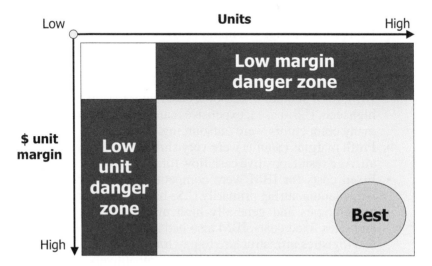

FIGURE 6.9. Strategic path: Positive cash flow map.

the strategic path. This could include the management of manufacturing capacity in terms of cost controls and the management of market share with competitive strategy and price management. Equally important are managing price and variable costs together. Too often price is managed totally separate from variable costs by different people in the company, with different objectives in mind, and with different understanding of the cash flow dynamic.

A spectacular example of the low margin danger zone is the current situation facing IBM in their personal computer (PC) strategic paths. A recent press release from Lenovo announces their acquisition of the IBM PC Division.[1] In this case, IBM has decided to sell off the division because they cannot generate positive net cash flow from this strategic path. Looking at their entire cash flow dynamic, no simple, single cause of the problem exists. However, a major component of the problem is IBM's low unit margins ($/PC) on this strategic path. For IBM, PCs were in the low margin danger zone.

Looking at the cash flow dynamic, some important features of IBM's PC strategic paths were the following:

- Unit PC sales were reasonably strong, despite the fact that IBM fell to third place in the market behind Dell and Hewlett-Packard.
- Unit prices through the market networks for PCs were under severe competitive pressures across most of the major PC market segments, for example, from Dell.
- Unit variable costs were too high, and likely noncompetitive for IBM, for a number of reasons. One major reason was the use of high tech, U.S.-based, expensive manufacturing processes when many competitors were outsourcing.
- Profit margins ($/unit) were very slim for IBM, if any existed at all. As a result, positive cash flow for PCs was very low, if at all.
- Fixed costs for IBM were competitively comparatively high, with manufacturing primarily U.S.-based, backward-integrated, technologies and generally high manufacturing, distribution, and sales fixed costs. IBM also had a huge and expensive sales and logistics infrastructure to pay for.
- Capital investments for IBM were competitively high, with the attendant high negative cash flows necessary to sustain them.

- With all the previous competitive factors in place, IBM likely had a negative or very low net cash flow situation.

These net cash flow effects do not arise from one single strategic factor. They reflect the ability of an entire strategic path, with all its interactions, to create net cash flow.

THE LOW UNITS DANGER ZONE

The low units danger zone defines strategic path opportunities that have significant unit margins but relatively low unit sales. A relatively small decline in unit sales or market share can result in a devastating drop in positive cash flow. In this danger zone, emphasis has to be on the management of market share and unit sales. Strategies for low unit sales strategic paths are very different than strategies for low margin paths. In these cases, market share and size of market segments accessed are the critical variables that should be addressed in marketing plans. These variables are the major drivers of unit sales the major sensitivity variables in these situations.

Major examples of the low units danger zone are the strategic paths of AECL (Atomic Energy of Canada Limited) in the nuclear power plants business, with the CANDU nuclear reactor. The cash flow profiles have a huge sensitivity to unit sales for the following reasons:

- Unit sales in the global market for nuclear power plants are very low in general, and have huge fluctuations.
- Unit prices are very competitive and difficult to compare to competitors, with complex, long-term financing operation and service deals requiring huge investments and complex negotiations.
- Unit variable costs are very high and unpredictable, occurring over long time periods, in many cases, years. Since each reactor is really a "one-off" (custom made), frequently no substantive learning-curve effect can occur.
- Unit margins could be estimated to be theoretically high, but dwindle over the long development times, even potentially turning negative.

- The technologies bundles in a reactor are very complex, with many choices; are difficult to integrate; and are frequently changing over the long product development cycle. This can dramatically increase variable costs.
- As a result of the previous factors, positive cash flows in the situation are very sensitive to unit sales.
- The negative cash flows, fixed costs, and investments are extremely high over very long time periods. They are also very uncertain and prone to escalate because of the time and technical complexity involved. In addition, winning competitive bidding deals for power plants often involves financing of customers negative cash flows, which introduces other negative cash flows for AECL.

As a result of all these complex and interacting factors, strategic paths are very sensitive to unit sales for AECL. In addition, the choice of technologies in the complex bundle for a nuclear power plant can have a great impact on cash flows.

It is useful in the marketing planning process to separate strategic paths into those that are in the best zone, the low margin danger zone and the low unit danger zone, and for the management team managing these strategic paths to understand the differences for marketing and strategic planning.

EXPLORING SENSITIVITIES IN FIXED COSTS AND INVESTMENTS

It is clear that the critical success factor in existing and new strategic-path opportunities is their capacity to create net cash flow. Until positive cash flow generation is under some kind of clear management, it makes little sense to attack fixed costs and investments. In the worst case, if a strategic path cannot be managed and planned to produce significant positive cash flow, reducing fixed costs and investments is not going to have a significant effect on net cash flow. In the other extreme, an extraordinarily high positive cash flow producing strategic path has great capacity for significant increases in net cash flow if fixed costs and investments are better managed.

The Impact of Fixed Cost Sensitivities

Fixed costs (negative cash flows), their sensitivity, and their movement over time should be a critical part of managing the plan for a strategic path. They should be particularly watched when changing the fixed cost structure impacts on the positive cash flow generation of a strategic path. One of the great dangers in the cash flow dynamic is allocating unrelated fixed costs to a strategic path. This frequently occurs. Having said this, if positive cash flow for a strategic path can be grown significantly, fixed cost management can produce a high degree of leverage in cash flow creation.

The critical question that has to be asked is, "If we need certain levels of fixed costs to enhance cash flow, will that affect other dimensions of the cash flow dynamic for the strategic path, such as market share, segment size accessed, price, variable cost, or other factors?" These effects can be well hidden and are important to explore in detail.

The Impact of Investment Sensitivities

Investment sensitivities are particularly relevant in marketing planning for new strategic path opportunities. Once investment levels have been estimated, the critical question is not the level of revenues that the investment will produce but the level of positive cash flow that it will produce and its timing. At that point, the question has to be asked if different investment levels for a strategic path and their financial structure (debt, equity) can have a significant impact on net cash flow.

The Critical Technologies Investments

In this book, the complexity and difficulty of choosing and bundling the best technologies has been made clear. Because it is often by far the highest investment over the longest and most uncertain time horizon, its investment emerges as the most sensitive factor in the net cash flow performance of the venture and therefore its success. For a number of reasons, estimating and managing the investments in new technologies represents a special problem.

Frequently, the technologies are new and their bundling unique for a particular product functionality. The investment estimates can be very speculative and uncertain. In addition, the timing of the investments can be very unclear, and can have a huge effect on the cash flow profiles.

THE CRITICAL IMPORTANCE
OF MARKET NETWORK ADOPTION RATES

The importance of adoption rate to the cash flow dynamic has been outlined in this book. Adoption rates for new strategic paths are notoriously inaccurate; unit sales frequently occur much later and are much lower than anticipated. This is often a major contributor to negative cash flows and failure. However, in addition to adoption rate, all of the other variables in the cash flow dynamic can cause major upsets in cash flow projections, including market segment size, price, variable costs, margins, fixed costs, and investments.

All of these factors in the cash flow dynamic and their interactions must be dynamically analyzed, simulated, and tracked in their behavior over time in order to manage the potential success for a new strategic path.

Adoption rate through the market networks for a strategic path will be driven to a large degree by the cash flow creation capacity of the strategic path for the other key members of the market network. To explore and analyze this critical factor we need the concept of strategic leverage.

What Is Strategic Leverage?

For any company in the market network considering adoption or bundling of your strategic path, *strategic leverage* is the ratio of strategic payoffs (positive cash flows) the company derives from adoption compared to the resources (negative cash flows) committed to the adoption. This is shown conceptually in Figure 6.10. A high-leverage strategic path is one for which customers' payoffs (positive cash flows) are very high and resources (negative cash flows) required to adopt very low. Strategic payoffs are defined in terms of the customer's cash flow dynamic. This cash flow dynamic represents, in simple terms, how each of the companies in the market network gen-

For any company in your market network to adopt a new strategic path, maximizing the ratio:

Strategic Payoffs from Adoption (Positive Cash Flow Impact)

Resources Committed (Negative Cash Flow Impact)

FIGURE 6.10. The concept of strategic leverage.

erates net cash flow from adopting your strategic path and integrating it with their own.

Your path can have an impact on market share in the markets in which they compete, the size of the segments in which they compete, the price and variable cost relationships and margin they enjoy, or their fixed costs and investment structure. In rejecting competitive strategic paths and choosing yours, the most powerful incentive for market network members to choose you is the leverage you create for their cash flow dynamic. As noted earlier, this is the most important reason for you to analyze and understand the sensitivities in all the cash flow dynamics of companies in your market network that will be critical in the adoption.

Identifying Points of Strategic Leverage

For any other member of your market network, adoption of a strategic path can have any or all of the following points of leverage. This is shown conceptually in Figure 6.11, in which the market network and its members are seen as a network of cash flow dynamics.

1. *Market-share leverage:* Adoption of your strategic path enables your customers to significantly increase their market share on their strategic paths.
2. *Market-size leverage:* Adoption enables customers to pursue strategic paths that are significantly larger in size.
3. *Unit leverage:* Adoption enables customers to significantly increase unit sales for their products.
4. *Price leverage:* Adoption enables customers to significantly change the price for their products.
5. *Variable-cost leverage:* Adoption enables customers to significantly reduce the unit variable cost for their products.
6. *Unit-margin leverage:* Adoption enables customers to significantly increase the unit margin for their products.
7. *Fixed-cost leverage:* Adoption enables customers to significantly reduce the fixed-cost base for their strategic paths.
8. *Investment leverage:* Adoption enables customers to significantly reduce the investment base for their strategic paths.
9. *Interactive leverage:* Adoption of your strategic path has an interactive effect on two or more points of leverage in the situation. For example, adoption may increase customers' market share and market size so that the combined effect produces much greater strategic leverage than either point of leverage acting independently.

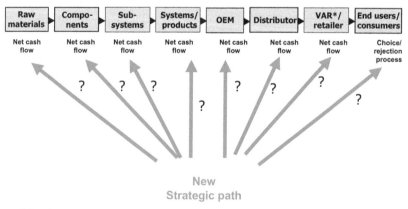

FIGURE 6.11. Market networks strategic leverage.

Impact on Market Network Adoption Rates

The major reason for you to carefully analyze strategic-leverage creation in your market networks is its potential impact on adoption rates for your strategic path, which is one of the most sensitive factors that influences potential net cash flow. Adoption rates will be faster for a new product when greater creation of strategic leverage occurs. Adoption rates will be higher

- When more points of strategic leverage can be created for each particular company in your market network. In the extreme, a new strategic path could have an impact on all the cash flow drivers: market share, market size, units, price, variable cost, unit margins, fixed costs, and investments.
- When higher-impact points of leverage can be created, then the impact of the new strategic path on a particular cash flow driver becomes highly sensitive and significant in magnitude.
- When strategic leverage can be created for more companies in your market network.
- When higher-impact points of leverage can be created between different types of companies in the market network.

The major objective of strategic-leverage analysis is to explore how it can be created in the market network for a particular strategic path, and how this will influence adoption rate.

Strategic-Leverage Zones

Another concept for exploring strategic leverage for a member of your market network is shown in Figure 6.12. Strategic-leverage zones organize strategic paths on the basis of their impact on different network members positive and negative cash flow impact. As shown, for a network member company, the "A" zone features a high positive impact on the member's positive cash flow, with little impact on their negative cash flow. This is a high strategic leverage situation. The reverse is true of the "C" zone. It is important to note that the impact of these zones can be estimated with real number data.

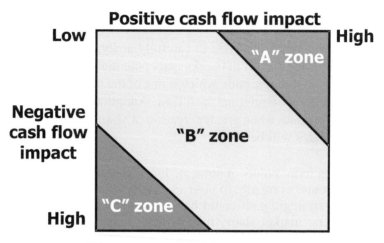

FIGURE 6.12. Strategic leverage zones.

ESTIMATING STRATEGIC-PATH CASH FLOWS

It is important to explore a detailed case example to illustrate the connections between the critical strategic path choices and their impact on net cash flows. In this case, synthetic blood will be used.

A Case Example: Biopure

It is important to explore the net cash flow characteristics of a strategic path with a detailed and specific real case example. The example here is that of Biopure Corporation.[2] Biopure's future depended on two new "blood substitutes": Oxyglobin for the veterinary market and Hemopure for the human market. Though based on similar new molecular technologies, the two opportunities represented totally different strategic paths, with very different cash flow characteristics.

An Overview of Biopure

Biopure Corporation was founded in 1984 as a privately owned biopharmaceutical firm specializing in the technologies of purification of proteins for human and veterinary use. By 1998, these technologies had taken Biopure to the point where it was one of three legitimate contenders in the emerging field of blood substitutes. Blood substitutes were designed to replicate the oxygen-carrying function of actual blood while eliminating the shortcomings associated with the transfusion of donated blood. Through the end of 1997, no blood substitute had received approval for use anywhere in the world.

Biopure's entries into this field were Hemopure for the human market and Oxyglobin for the animal market. Both products consisted of the oxygen-carrying protein hemoglobin, that had been removed from red blood cells, purified to eliminate infectious agents, and chemically modified to increase its safety and effectiveness. What distinguished Hemopure and Oxyglobin from other hemoglobin-based blood substitutes under development was that they were bovine-sourced as opposed to human-sourced; they were derived from the blood of cattle. To date, Biopure had invested more than $200 million in the development of Oxyglobin and Hemopure and in the construction of a state-of-the-art manufacturing facility.

Both of Biopure's products fell under the approval process of the United States government's Food and Drug Administration (FDA), which required that each product be proven safe and effective for medical use. Oxyglobin received final FDA approval for commercial release as a veterinary blood substitute, and Hemopure soon entered Phase 3 clinical trials and was optimistically expected to see final FDA approval for release as a human blood substitute sometime in 1999.

Human Blood Supply and Demand

Fourteen million units of red blood cells (RBCs) were donated in 1995 in the United States. Approximately 12.9 million of these units came from individuals who voluntarily donated to one of more than 1,000 nonprofit blood collection organizations. By far, the largest of these organizations was the American Red Cross, which collected half of all the blood donated in the United States in 1995 through a network of 44 regional blood collection centers. Typically, the Red Cross and the other blood collection organizations supported "bloodmobiles," which traveled to high schools, colleges, and places of employment to reach potential donors. The remaining 1.1 million units of RBCs were autologous donations made directly to a hospital blood center.

Given the low rate of donation and the relatively short shelf life of RBCs it was not uncommon for medical facilities and blood banks to experience periodic shortages of RBCs. This was especially true during the winter holidays and the summer months, periods that routinely displayed both increased demand and decreased rates of donation.

Of the 14 million units of RBCs donated in 1995, 2.7 million were discarded due to contamination or expiration (units older than six weeks). Another 3.2 million units were transfused into 1.5 million patients who suffered from chronic anemia, an ongoing deficiency in the oxygen-carrying ability of the blood. The remaining 8.1 million units were transfused into 2.5 million patients who suffered from acute blood loss brought on by elective surgeries, emergency surgeries, or trauma.

The Veterinary Blood Market

The product functionality of RBCs for animals is biologically similar to its role for humans: RBCs transport oxygen to an animal's tissues and organs. In practice, however, the availability and transfusion of blood is considerably more constrained in the veterinary market than it is in the human market. Approximately 15,000 small-animal veterinary practices existed in the United States in 1995. Of course, about 95 percent were primary care practices, which provided preventative care (e.g., shots, checkups), routine treatment of illness (e.g., infections, chronic anemia), and limited emergency care or specialty care practices. Approximately 75 percent of primary care practices referred some or all of their major surgery and severe trauma cases to emergency care practices.

Human Blood Substitutes

Originally conceived as a vehicle to treat wounded soldiers in battlefield settings, the potential for a human blood substitute for nonmilitary use became increasingly apparent after the 1950s. This period saw a significant rise in auto accidents, the advent of open-heart and organ-transplant surgeries, and the AIDS crisis, which called into question the safety of the blood supply.

By 1998, several companies appeared to be on the verge of a viable blood substitute with a class of product called *hemoglobin-based blood substitutes*. These products attempted to exploit the natural oxygen-carrying capabilities of hemoglobin while eliminating the limitations associated with donated RBCs. Each of these companies was attempting to (1) extract the hemoglobin found within human or animal RBCs, (2) purify that hemoglobin to eliminate infectious agents, and (3) modify the otherwise unstable free hemoglobin molecule to prevent it from breaking down. These purification and modification processes were nontrivial and represented the bulk of blood-substitute research conducted over the past twenty years.

Animal Blood Substitutes

Through early 1998, Biopure was the only company that was actively engaged in the development of a blood substitute for the small-animal veterinary market. Although little existed to prevent competitors (or anyone else) from attempting to enter the veterinary market, any company wishing to do so would have to initiate an FDA-approval process specific to the veterinary market. By one estimate, assuming a company immediately began such a process, it would take two to five years to bring a product to market.

Status of Hemopure. As of early 1998, Hemopure was in Phase 3 clinical trials in Europe, with FDA approval for Phase 3 trials in the United States appearing imminent. In anticipation of this approval, Biopure had established sites for Phase 3 trials and was ready to proceed immediately upon approval. Acknowledging the potential pitfalls of any clinical trials, Biopure remained confident that the Phase 3 trials would be successful and that the FDA would grant full approval sometime in 1999. Biopure expected to commercially release Hemopure sometime in late 1999.

In line with the anticipated price of competitors, Biopure planned to price Hemopure at $600 to $800 per unit. However, little systematic testing had been done by Biopure to determine the acceptability of these prices. In particular, little was known of the price sensitivity of medical personnel, insurance providers, or of patients when it came to human blood substitutes.

Status of Oxyglobin. In 1997, Biopure established the Veterinary Products Division and hired Andy Wright to oversee the marketing and sale of Oxyglobin. Working under the assumption that Biopure would begin selling Oxyglobin immediately upon approval, Wright faced a host of decisions, including how to price and how to distribute Oxyglobin. Supporting him in these decisions was a team of seven employees: one director of marketing, one technical service representative (to support ordering and billing), and three sales representatives (to make sales calls and generate orders).

The Oxyglobin Strategic Path

The Oxyglobin strategic path is shown in Figure 6.13. This summarizes the critical strategic-focus choices of technologies, product functionalities, market networks, and end-user segments. As shown, a wide range of strategic choices exists within each area along with a large number of potential different bundles for focus. The technologies are complex, with many potential bundles, both on the product, process, and supply-side technologies. The product functionalities bundles present many alternative bases for strategic focus, depending on different end-user segments. The market networks present a major challenge for bundling focus, with many different logistical, information, and distribution routes to different types of veterinarians and an-

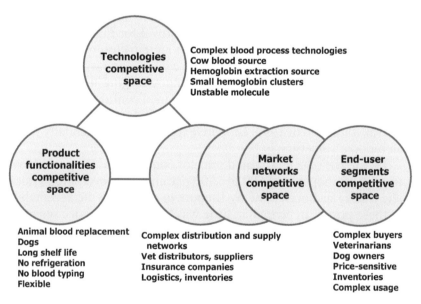

FIGURE 6.13. Strategic paths: Biopure Oxyglobin.

imal clinics. Very different end-user segments exist, with different potential perceptions and applications for blood substitutes.

Each of the four major choices for strategic focus presented a major challenge for Biopure. But a far greater problem is integrating the four strategic bundles into a coherent focused strategy.

The Hemopure Strategic Path

The Hemopure strategic path is shown in Figure 6.14. As in the case of Oxyglobin, each of the four major strategic choices presents a complex potential bundle with many possible strategic combinations. The technologies bundle is similar to Oxyglobin, except the small molecules have to be removed, which halves the initial plant capacity. As will be shown in the cash flow profiles, this has a huge impact on net cash flow. For the product functionalities bundle, a large number of focused bundles are possible, depending on the end-user segment and how you choose to position the product. The market network for Hemopure is totally separate and different from that for Oxyglobin. It is also much more complex and difficult to penetrate. For the end-

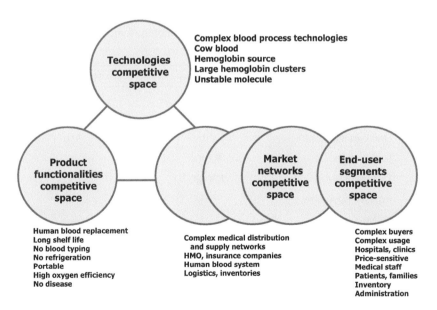

FIGURE 6.14. Strategic paths: Biopure Hemopure.

user segments, the human application for synthetic blood is much more complex than for animals.

What makes this case so interesting is that, although the two possible strategic paths seem similar, they are radically different and represent very different strategic focus. They represent a very tough set of strategic choices. A critical criterion for the choice of strategic focus will be the cash flow estimates and profiles.

Initial Estimates of Cash Flow
for Oxyglobin and Hemopure

An initial rough estimate of net cash flows for the two alternative strategic paths is shown in Table 6.1. This is a simple initial set of estimates using the cash flow dynamic outlined in this book. As shown, at the initial full-plant capacity, a huge difference in net cash flow performance exists between the Oxyglobin and Hemopure strategic paths. Under these simple conditions, the estimates show a net cash loss of $8 million per year for Oxyglobin, and a positive net cash flow of $53 million per year for Hemopure. This is not a basis for a fast conclusion for the managers involved of what strategic path to pur-

TABLE 6.1. Biopure: Comparative cash flow estimates for Oxyglobin and Hemopure at full initial capacity.

Cash flow	Oxyglobin	Hemopure
Positive		
Unit price	$200	$800
Unit variable cost	$10	$10
Unit margin	$190	$790
Unit sales	$300K	$150K
Positive cash flow	$57M	$118M
Negative		
Fixed costs	$25M	$25M
Investments	$200M	$200M
Investments × 0.2	$40M	$40M
Negative cash flow	$65M	$65M
Net	($8M)	$53M

sue, but it clearly raises some tough questions. It appears that Oxyglobin is likely to create negative cash flow, at least at initial plant capacity. To pursue these questions, the detailed cash flow profile tool outlined in the Management Application Toolkit can be applied.

It is important to note how critical it is to conceptualize these cash flow profiles as fast, fluid, experimental, iterative estimates rather than highly analytic, precise, one-shot calculations. Testing a new set of estimates should take only a few minutes.

Oxyglobin: Detailed Cash Flow Profile Estimates

Detailed cash flow estimates for the Oxyglobin strategic path are shown in Table 6.2. These estimates are for the first ten years of a strategic path. As shown, with these estimates, this Oxyglobin strategic path seems to be a tough situation, with negative net cash flows. This means that different strategic paths will have to be explored for Oxyglobin. In this case, it would most likely mean different end-user segments and different market networks that would require more plant capacity, and to be brought on faster. As the profile shows, the net cash losses for the initial strategic path may be initially huge as the plant capacity of 300,000 units/year comes on stream.

Hemopure: Detailed Cash Flow Profile Estimates

Detailed cash flow estimates for the Hemopure strategic path are shown in Table 6.3. As shown, with this set of estimates, Hemopure seems to have a vastly better strategic path than Oxyglobin. A small net cash loss occurs in the first year, followed by high and growing positive net cash flow.

SUMMARY

It is important to pull together some of the many potential bundle choices on a strategic path that can cause severe problems in the net cash flow performance. Some examples of these potentially negative impacts are summarized in Figure 6.15. These are merely a few significant examples of how these four critical strategic choices can impact net cash flow. Any one factor in itself has the potential to turn net

TABLE 6.2. Biopure: Oxyglobin cash flow profile estimates.

Cash flow	Year									
	1	2	3	4	5	6	7	8	9	10
Positive										
Unit price	200	200	200	200	200	200	200	200	200	200
Unit variable cost	10	10	10	10	10	10	10	10	10	10
Unit margin	190	190	190	190	190	190	190	190	190	190
Unit sales (000s)	100	120	140	180	200	240	280	300	300	300
Positive cash flow (000s)	19,000	22,800	26,600	34,200	38,000	45,600	53,200	57,000	57,000	57,000
Negative (000s)										
Fixed costs	25,000	25,000	25,000	25,000	25,000	25,000	25,000	25,000	25,000	25,000
Investments	200,000	200,000	200,000	200,000	200,000	200,000	200,000	200,000	200,000	200,000
Investments × 20 percent	40,000	40,000	40,000	40,000	40,000	40,000	40,000	40,000	40,000	40,000
Negative	65,000	65,000	65,000	65,000	65,000	65,000	65,000	65,000	65,000	65,000
Net	(46,000)	(42,200)	(38,400)	(30,800)	(27,000)	(19,400)	(11,800)	(8,000)	(8,000)	(8,000)
Cumulative	(46,000)	(88,200)								

————high negative net cash flow————

Note: All table entries are in dollars.

178

TABLE 6.3. Biopure: Hemopure cash flow profile estimates.

Cash flow	Year									
	1	2	3	4	5	6	7	8	9	10
Positive										
Unit price	800	800	800	800	800	800	800	800	800	800
Unit variable cost	10	10	10	10	10	10	10	10	10	10
Unit margin	790	790	790	790	790	790	790	790	790	790
Unit sales (000s)	80	100	110	120	130	140	150	150	150	150
Positive cash flow (000s)	63,200	79,000	86,900	94,800	102,700	110,600	118,500	118,500	118,500	118,500
Negative (000s)										
Fixed costs	25,000	25,000	25,000	25,000	25,000	25,000	25,000	25,000	25,000	25,000
Investments	200,000	200,000	200,000	200,000	200,000	200,000	200,000	200,000	200,000	200,000
Investments × 20 percent	40,000	40,000	40,000	40,000	40,000	40,000	40,000	40,000	40,000	40,000
Negative cash flow	65,000	65,000	65,000	65,000	65,000	65,000	65,000	65,000	65,000	65,000
Net cash flow	(1,800)	14,000	21,900	29,800	37,700	45,600	53,500	53,500	53,500	53,500
Cumulative cash flow	(1,800)	12,200	34,100	63,900	101,600	147,200	200,700	254,200	307,700	361,200

Notes: All table entries are in dollars. Parentheses indicate negative net cash flow.

	Impact on positive cash flow	Impact on negative cash flow
Technologies	Technologies bundle inflates variable costs Technologies bundle complex, difficult to manufacture Appeals only to a small end-user segment Difficult for end users to understand Has risks in use Won't support high price Not backward-compatible	Technologies bundle inflates investments Manufacturing investments too high Technologies bundle inflates fixed costs Technologies too complex Parts, servicing costs too high
Functionalities	Functionality not great Little functionality differentiation Difficult for end user to utilize End user can't integrate functionality Not backward-compatible Difficult to understand differentiation	Complex functionality inflates investments Complex functionality inflates fixed costs High training costs High service costs
Networks	Complex, difficult for network companies to manage Low margins for network companies Logistics too complex Difficult access to end-user companies Integration with other technologies difficult	High Ssrvice costs for network companies High logistics costs High training costs High inventory costs
Segments	Segment too small Segment slow to reject current functionality Slow segment adoption rate Segment has financial constraints Functionality differentiation doesn't fit segment	Segment can't support investments Segment can't support fixed costs Segment expensive to access Selling costs too high Service, support costs too high

(Left vertical label: Strategic path choices)

FIGURE 6.15. Strategic paths: Factors reducing net cash flow.

cash flow negative. Taken in combinations, they can have a potentially devastating impact.

This underscores the importance of teams analyzing strategic paths in their totality rather than in separate parts. Looking at Figure 6.15, the importance of the transformation teams becomes obvious. For the technologies team, the choices can have the impacts shown through both positive and negative cash flows. These cash flow impacts can occur alone or in combination with others. Looking at Figure 6.15, it is easy to see the potential cash flow impact of several of these factors "going the wrong way" because of poor management. The potential impact of some major factors in product functionalities, market networks, and end-user segments are also shown.

CRITICAL QUESTIONS FOR MANAGERS

The following key questions should be asked and resolved definitively with respect to the cash flow dynamic:

- Are your net cash flow objectives clear? It is critical throughout a new strategic path to have clear and widely shared operational estimates of net cash flow objectives and realities. Managers and management teams frequently proceed down a new strategic path with widely divergent concepts of what the financial objectives are, or, for that matter, have no shared financial objectives at all. Equally important is the operationality of objectives. The measures, the units, and the basis for gathering net cash flow estimates should be clearly defined.

- Where are the greatest net cash flow sensitivities? Is it clear on which of the major cash flow drivers are going to have the greatest impact on overall profitability for the opportunity?
- Are market and end-user segment share estimates realistic with respect to the size of the market segment being attacked and competitive reactions?
- What is the minimum market share you will need for the opportunity to merely survive and break even?
- What is the maximum market share you might get out of the best of circumstances? The critical question here is, How realistic are your market share estimates?
- How large is the actual end-user segment of the market on which you are focusing after correcting for distribution intensity and for the exact segments that you are positioned against?
- Are market segment sizes realistic? Do they match competitive measures? How much might they grow over time?
- Are adoption-rate estimates realistic? Do they account for all the possible lags in the market networks and in the competitive situations and reactions that might significantly slow adoption by buyers?
- Are adoption-rate estimates consistent with the choice/rejection process of the customers sought?
- Do adoption-rate estimates take recognition of the strategic leverage developed for market network members?
- Do prices for the new product make sense when you look at the expected adoption rate and competitive differentiation, pricing, and pressures?
- Are prices likely to have a significant impact on improving buyer choice/rejection and on indicating rapid adoption of the new product?
- Are prices consistent with the unit variable cost and unit margin projections?

- Are unit variable cost estimates realistic in terms of long-run manufacturing and supply of the product?
- How do your variable costs compare to competitive variable costs? Is there competitive differentiation?
- When variable costs are coupled with price, are they consistent with unit margin projections?
- Are unit margins significant and realistic over the short run for the new strategic path?
- Are unit margins tied to price and variable costs estimates that are believable and achievable?
- Are unit margins high enough to produce significant positive cash flow creation in the opportunity?
- What factors might significantly change unit margins in the short run?
- Are the fixed costs associated with the overall strategy for the product realistic?
- Are all costs taken into account clearly? Are they real?
- Are investments and development costs realistic in terms of the amount and time they are likely to take?
- How much of the fixed costs are tied up in various investments in the new product?
- How well can the investments be controlled?
- Is the cash flow dynamic brought together in one place and constantly scrutinized by the entire management team?
- Has the cash flow dynamic for the opportunity been brought together clearly with all the numbers and estimates in one place so that everyone on the management teams can see them all at once and test the sensitivities?
- Is the cash flow dynamic available in such a way that people can change their estimates, look at changes quickly, and see their significance with respect to the overall net cash flow of the opportunity?
- Is the cash flow dynamic constantly revised to reflect the latest realities, for example, an increase in variable costs, or investments, or a later market introduction? The most critical issue is if it becomes clear that the opportunity has gone from a positive net cash flow to negative, is the team able to think seriously about backing away from the opportunity and saying no?

- Is the relative net cash flow for different strategic paths clear and valid? When you look at the cash flow dynamic for a particular strategic path are you comparing it clearly to other places the resources might go? (The Biopure case is an excellent example.)
- Are the cash flow dynamics of other strategic paths as visible as the cash flow dynamics for this particular path? Are they compared by the same people at the same time so you can make choices about resource allocations?
- Are all the cash flow dynamics carefully scrutinized for their validity so that management teams can allocate resources for strategic paths in which the cash flow estimates are simply unrealistic?
- Do all key functional teams and managers have a shared understanding of relative net cash flows?
- Do all the key functional teams have the same information on the relative net cash flows of different new and existing strategic paths?
- Does everyone in the organization know who the "stars" are and from where the net cash flows are coming? If twenty percent of your strategic paths currently produce eighty percent of the net cash flows, do all managers in the organization know which ones they are? If a new strategic path is going to account for thirty percent of your net cash flow, does everybody in the organization know why and have the numbers clearly in front of them? Is there a shared understanding in the organizations of who the winners and losers are? This is critically important.
- Has the strategic leverage for the market networks been carefully analyzed? Has the cash flow impact for all market network members been thoroughly analyzed to spot barriers to rapid adoption and cash flow generation?

Chapter 7

Managing Strategic Paths: Creating Project and Transformation Teams

INTRODUCTION

The concept of strategic paths has the potential to be powerful in helping managers achieve strategic focus for specific new technology and product opportunities. It is designed around four major strategic bundles for market focus: technologies focus, product functionalities focus, market networks focus, and end-user segments focus. By teams of managers carefully mapping these areas onto each other and working through the process, companies can ensure that great strategic synergies and competitive differentiation can be developed. The ultimate objective for this strategic-path management is to create and sustain high and growing net cash flow.

However, these positive conditions in the process can only take place if managers in the company recognize the need for a set of team and organizational processes to ensure that managers actually focus on cash flow, with real toughness and candor. This requires a combination of culturally engrained understanding about what market focus means and creating the appropriate teams and management structures to carefully pursue highly focused strategic paths.

UNDERSTANDING THE COMPETITIVE POWER OF MARKET FOCUS

It is critically important that all functional managers involved in the process of developing new technologies and products have a shared and culturally engrained understanding of the competitive power of market focus. Market focus demands making tough choices in the four critical areas that are never easy to make.

- First, focus of technologies: creating an evolving technologies bundle that has the potential to create and sustain high competitive differentiation.
- Second, focus in product functionalities: creating product functionalities bundles that create high competitive differentiation.
- Third, clear focus in market networks, in all their complexity, so that they have the individual and collective capacity to deliver the differentiated strategic path to the end-user segment.
- Fourth, focus on specific end-user segments that are clearly defined.

Market focus can occur only if all four of these areas are clearly focused and intensely managed. Failure in one means failure in all. More important, powerful market focus can be created only if the focus in one strategic bundle builds and supports focus in others. Too often in organizations market focus is seen by functional managers as focus within a particular area rather than across strategic choices.

THE NEED FOR STRATEGIC-PATH INTEGRATION

As previously outlined, market focus can happen only if strategic path integration occurs along with management of the transformation processes. Without integration, focus simply can't happen. This is easy to say, but very difficult for managers to do. Frequently, the managers making the strategic choices in technologies, product functionalities, market networks, and end-user segments are different managers located in different places. They tend to manage the individual critical strategic-path choices independently. Not only that, but the choices tend to come along temporally, in some kind of sequence, so they're never brought together at any particular point in time.

Managing the Four Critical Strategic-Path Choices

The need for strategic-path integration has been outlined. At the same time, a great need to manage the four critical strategic-path choices as bundles in and of themselves exists. The managers involved have to work between clearly managing the four individual areas of choice and working with other managers, in teams, to try to get strategic-path integration.

The Critical Organizational Processes

Some of the critical conditions for ensuring a coherent and highly synergistic strategic path have been briefly discussed. A number of organizational processes are critically important in making this happen.

Creating Functionally Integrated Project Teams

The importance of multifunctional project teams in managing new technologies and product development has been stressed in much of the management literature. This book emphasizes and magnifies the importance of these project teams, and within them develops the concept of transformational teams. The only way companies can get the creation of differentiation, focus, integration, and synergy across the four critical choices on a strategic path is if clear, organizational mechanisms make it happen.

MANAGING PROJECT TEAMS: CREATING FOCUSED TRANSFORMATION TEAMS

The power of multifunctional teams to manage new technology and product projects and opportunities is well-documented. Many advantages to having these teams exist. The strategic-path concept presents an opportunity to further focus these teams around the four major strategic decisions contained on a strategic path. As shown in Figure 7.1, each multifunctional project team can be further focused into four transformation teams: a technology team, a product-functionality team, a market-segment team, and a market-network team.

This enables the project team to get the advantages of integration while at the same time sustaining and retaining functional focus. However, the transformation teams are not focused functionally but are made up of subgroups of the project team who have an interest, in-

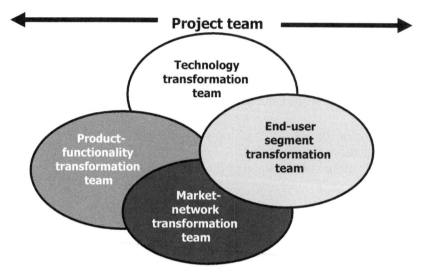

FIGURE 7.1. The formation of focused transformation teams.

volvement, and passion for their particular set of strategic choices. It is entirely possible, for example, for one person to be a member of more than one of the transformation teams.

The Technology-Transformation Team

The technology team focuses their attention primarily on the physical technologies bundle being developed on the strategic path and its potential impact on the other three strategic bundles: product functionalities, market networks, and end-user segments. This responsibility, however, doesn't end with just the technologies involved in the company itself. It must include the impact of all technologies, both on the supply side and market side of the product functionality bundle for the customer. The team's focus and concern has got to be on any opportunities or problems, or positives or negatives related to the entire bundle of technologies that will have an impact on the success of the product, including all of those entailed in after-sales service. In many cases, this is a very broad spectrum with a great number of technologies involved and makes even clearer why the focus of the technologies team is so important.

The Product-Functionality Transformation Team

The focus of the product-functionality transformation team is on creating focused and differentiated product functionality directed at a specific market end-user segment and working very diligently to make sure that perceived product functionality (in the perception of the customer in the end-user segment) is what the customer needs and what can establish differentiation. It is vitally important, therefore, that the product-functionality transformation team see their role as quite different from the technology transformation team. The product-functionality team literally represents the perceptions of the customer. The strategic transformation between technology and product functionality takes place as a negotiated process rather than a process driven simply by what technologies are available to the team.

The Market-Segment Transformation Team

The market-segment team's primary responsibility and focus is on understanding and creating different segments of end users on which to focus. By enabling the team to focus on this, the effort on segmentation should go far beyond simply mapping existing segments of the market to looking for whole new ways to map and create new opportunities for customers that could be served by this particular strategic path.

The Market-Networks Transformation Team

The market-networks team focuses their attention on the entire process of bundling market network members from their company through to the end-user segments. As shown in the discussion of market networks in this book, this is an enormously complex task and benefits greatly from the focus of this particular transformation team. Both of the examples of car fuel cells and synthetic blood used in this book exemplify the complexity of these market networks in many competitive situations and the sheer number of strategic choices they represent for the companies involved.

Team Membership

The previous four transformation teams make up, in total, the entire project team. The team membership in each of these transformation teams should not be based on functional expertise alone but also on the desire of people to have different perspectives brought into the team. As the project team evolves, the membership in the transformation teams may also evolve as people discover their interest and their knowledge base and get used to what they like about the project. As more and more is found out about these four critical decision choices, membership may change on the basis of understanding and knowledge of critical decisions. The important thing is that it's a negotiated process, and that the teams are in constant contact through the overall team process but have significant time to pursue and get clear on their particular area of the four major strategic choices.

Transformation Team Interaction

Each of the transformation teams has a unique situational focus, as outlined. But each also has focused interactions with other transformation teams around the transformation processes. These interactions are shown in Table 7.1. As shown, each transformation team has three transformation processes that require intense, focused interaction with other teams. For example, as shown in Table 7.1, the technologies team needs to focus its attention on three transformation processes: T1 (technologies→product functionalities), T2 (technolo-

TABLE 7.1. Creating transformation teams: Roles, focus, and team interaction.

	Transformation team			
Transformation process	Technologies team	Product-functionalities team	Market-networks team	End-user segment team
T1	FOCUS	FOCUS		
T2	FOCUS		FOCUS	
T3	FOCUS			FOCUS
T4		FOCUS	FOCUS	
T5		FOCUS		FOCUS
T6			FOCUS	FOCUS

gies→market networks), and T3 (technologies→end-user segments). Enabling the technologies transformation team to focus on only these three transformation processes enables them to get a much deeper and more penetrating understanding of the management challenges and to be much more useful to the project team as a whole. The same is true of the other transformation teams.

Transformation Team Roles

Within the context of the overall project team, each of the transformation teams has the same set of fundamental roles. These roles are shown in Table 7.2, and are conceptualized in the following sections.

Expertise

Each transformation team is expected to have an evolving and growing set of in-depth substantive knowledge about their particular strategic area. For example, the technology team needs to keep the documentation of their cumulative understanding and knowledge of the technologies bundles to constantly raise questions among the project team and keep the project team advised of changes in the technologies. One of their critical roles is to make sure the project team

TABLE 7.2. Critical transformation team process roles.

Critical roles	Technology team	Product-functionality team	Market-network team	End-user segment team
Expertise				
Risk analysis				
Information/research				
Project process tracking				
Costs/cash flow tracking				
Hot zone creation				
Team negotiation				
Leadership				
Functional liaison				

has an open mind with respect to the changes in the components of the technologies bundle that can happen over the course of a project's development and market entry.

Risk Analysis and Communication

Each team is responsible for keeping track of and carefully analyzing the evolving set of risks that become evident as more and more information is gathered during the development of new technologies and their transformation into new products. Each of the four strategic bundles represents a different and complex set of risks, in themselves and in their impact on the six transformation processes. These need to be carefully tracked and shared with the project team.

Information Seeking and Research

Each transformation team, in response to the evolving set of risks it sees over the course of the project, needs to guide and conduct information seeking and research to respond to these risks in a thoughtful and analytical way. This can include the retention of consultants and market-research firms to actively do research to deal, on a continuing basis, with the changing set of risks. This information seeking will change over the course of the development of the technology and product, perhaps lasting over a period of years.

Project Process Tracking

Each of the transformation teams is responsible for managing its part of the process and integrating its process management with the other transformation teams. Frequently, changes will be picked up and analyzed by one transformation team that will have a dramatic impact on other transformation teams. These need to be continuously and immediately communicated and dealt with by the teams.

Costs and Cash Flow Tracking

Each team is responsible for tracking the impact of its strategic bundle on the cash flow dynamic of the project. This is a critically important activity. For example, the technology team may consider adopting a different new technology into its bundle that creates huge differentiation but may raise the variable manufacturing costs so much that it reduces the product functionality differentiation. The inclusion of that specific technology in the bundle then becomes a matter for strategic negotiation within the project team.

Creating Hot Zones: Negotiating with Other Teams

This is a critical activity for each one of the transformation teams. Within its own particular area, each transformation team has to be constantly looking for hot zones: areas of creative and powerful competitive differentiation within each one of the four major strategic bundles. Far more critical for each team is negotiating with other teams and making an effort to try and leverage differentiation within its own decision area to create differentiation in the other decision areas. The analysis to do this has been outlined in this book, but it is critically important that the members of the team do this. Much of it is creativity rather than analysis.

Leadership

Much has been written about leadership, and much of it does not fit reality very well. Here we will deal with the aspects of leadership that are specifically critical to the project and transformation teams in planning and managing strategic paths. Several important features of the strategic-path leadership process are as follows:

- The project and transformation team leaders must have really "bought in to" the net cash flow objective, and not just at the lip-service level.
- To make this operational, all of the leadership and the team members must have been educated to have a working knowledge of the cash flow dynamics and the pragmatic realities of how new strategic paths create net cash flow.
- To have real team leadership, the leaders and the entire team must all be clear on where they are trying to go and on what success really means for the project. This must be culturally shared and trusted, otherwise real team leadership is impossible.
- Transformation team members must see their objective as ensuring that their transformation process is not compromised by

all of the other strategic path choices and complexity that surrounds them. They must focus clearly on the critical aspects of the specific transformation processes for which they are responsible.

Functional Liaison

This is a very important role for each of the transformation teams. If possible, each of the teams should have at least one functional specialist peculiar to their area of choice. For example, for the technology transformation team, one manager on the team should be intimately familiar with the physical technologies.

The Importance of Real Teams

It is critically important for the management and creation of strategic paths to have, as closely as possible, "real" project and transformation teams, that is, teams that can actually operate with the distinctive advantages that teams and team effort can create. Frequently, groups of managers meet in a team environment but are not close to being a real team. What are some of the characteristics of a real team that are necessary to make strategic-path creation effective?

Team Self-Selection and Discipline

In dealing with strategic paths, transformation teams must have the discipline and self-selection empowerment to make sure that the team is working together, is brutally candid, and recognizes the importance of integrating the strategic-path choices. If members of the teams feel they really want to make some of these decisions unilaterally, without regard for the rest of the strategic path, then the team has to deal with that.

Compensation: Team Rewards versus Functional Group Rewards

Another critical condition for transformation teams has to do with the team rewarding and compensating its individual members, to some degree, on the success of the team with their strategic paths rather than only with functional group-based compensation. Too often, if, for example, an engineer is "seconded" to the technology team, and his or her compensation or rewards are not tied, to some degree, to the success of the team, the team may be compromised.

Clear and Shared Team Objectives

It is critically important for transformation teams to have a clear sense of the ultimate and overriding objective of cash flow over a reasonable time period and a clear sense of personal commitment and connectedness of net cash flow to their strategic choices along the strategic path.

Continuous Team Physical Proximity

Although it is not always possible, it is highly desirable for project and transformation teams to be physically available to each other so that the real process of continuously looking at these four critical areas of choice and their synergies is a human process rather than a database process.

Open Team Competition for Company Resources

It is very important that transformation teams see themselves as competing for the company resources to pursue their strategic path rather than just having the resources forever once they've been initially allocated. This internal company competitiveness matches the competitiveness they will meet in the market for their strategic paths, and even that which they will experience internally as they look at trade-offs within the strategic path.

CRITICAL QUESTIONS FOR MANAGERS

- What mechanisms do you have in place to integrate your technologies choices with the other major strategic choices for your new products?
- How do you cross the technology-market gap in your organization?

- Do you have teams organized to try to integrate these critical sets of strategic choices?
- How successful have your recent strategic paths been in net cash flow terms? Do you know?
- Can you connect specific managers and teams to greater success? Do you try?
- How do your different functional groups now plan and communicate regarding specific new technologies and their applications?
- Who leads your strategic processes in the choices of technologies, product functionalities, market networks, and end-user segments focus? Is it working?

Chapter 8

Creating Strategic Paths and Hot Zones: The Management Application Toolkit

INTRODUCTION

This book has presented a number of new concepts to help managers improve the integration and transformation of their complex technologies choices with three other critical strategic choices in competitive market strategies. An important part of this book is the presentation of this Management Application Toolkit. The Toolkit is a series of simple and powerful mapping processes that managers and transformation teams can use to explore specific strategic paths in a fast, simple, stepwise, iterative, and analytic way. These worksheets should be seen as a beginning of a continuous process in planning, managing, changing, and tracking strategic paths. In applying them, managers can create and use other new and existing worksheets in supporting analysis.

These worksheets are intended to be a tight, compact, and brief set of worksheets, because the reality of managers' lives is that they have scarce time working as teams to analyze. As a result, worksheets such as this must be brief, self-explanatory, and to the point. They must also be easy to use and understand.

Objectives

The objectives of this Management Application Toolkit are as follows:

- To enable teams of managers to make the most critical strategic connections between their technologies choices, product functionalities choices, market network choices, and end-user segment choices that can drive success.

- To help managers quickly create, explore, and test alternative new and modified strategic paths for new competitive opportunities.
- To help managers quickly recognize the risks, unknowns, and ambiguities for a strategic path to explore with effective and focused information gathering, research, and analysis.
- To help managers to quickly understand the critical strategic connections between technologies choices, product functionalities choices, market network choices, and end-user segment choices.
- To enable managers to quickly connect strategic paths to net cash flow creation, the most critical measure of new technology and new product success.
- To enable managers to quickly test the impact of changes in the four strategic path bundles on net cash flow.
- To help managers anticipate the strategic consequences of changes in technologies, product functionalities, market networks, and end-user segments.

Overview: The Toolkit Process

The toolkit process is shown in simple form in Figure 8.1. As shown, five fundamental iterative phases occur. These phases are intended to be brief and simple so that managers can initially focus on the concept of the strategic path rather than all of its detail. The phases are briefly described in the following sections.

The Phases

Phase One: Map the Strategic Path

The purpose of phase one is for the team to get as clear as possible on the strategic path to be explored and to map it carefully and in detail. This involves clearly identifying the major attributes of the technologies bundle, the product functionalities bundle, the market networks bundle, and the end-user segment bundles. It involves carefully describing them and identifying their critical individual characteristics. This phase is particularly crucial.

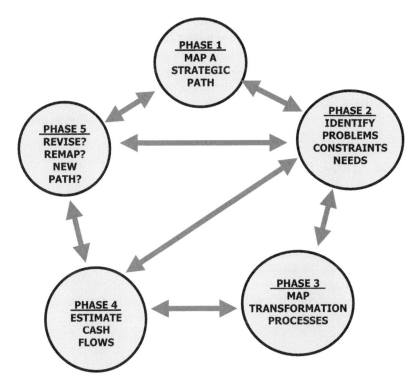

FIGURE 8.1. Application toolkit: Process overview.

Frequently, in discussing these types of situations with managers, it becomes clear that one of the major problems faced when planning new products and technologies is not being clear in sharing and communicating the choices they make on the strategic path. Frequently, in using Worksheet 8.1, the management team will have to iterate and rethink exactly the strategic path at which they are actually looking. By itself, this strategic clarification is a powerful outcome of phase one.

Phase Two: Identify Problems, Constraints,
and Information Needs

The importance of phase two is for the management team to use as they iterate through the strategic path process in order to continuously identify problems, constraints, and information needs with respect to clarifying them quickly. These issues can cover a wide range and are usually particular to each unique strategic path. Phase two should really be carried out after each set of worksheets as managers work through the other phases of the process.

What often happens in going through this phase is a stop in the team process when the team needs clarifying information to even proceed with the process.

Phase Three: Map Transformation Processes

Phase three is a series of maps that allow managers to map each of the critical four strategic bundles against the other bundles, trying to create hot zones. Managers are looking for these hot zones to create focused differentiation and synergy across the six key transformation processes on the strategic path. To help them, the series of maps allows managers to focus on two of the major strategic bundles at a time. Then, other maps help them to integrate the bundles into a coherent strategic path.

Phase Four: Estimate Net Cash Flows

Phase four is perhaps the most critical of the four phases. No matter how early it is in the creation and management of a strategic path, it is critical to make rough estimates of the cash flows that it creates. The key question is, "Does this strategic path really have the chance to produce any net cash flow?" This phase in the process has some very simple worksheets that allow managers to make simple, quick cash flow estimates.

Phase Five: Revise and Remap the Strategic Path

Phase five really occurs at each iteration of looking at strategic paths. It asks managers to consider changes along the strategic path with the need to completely remap the strategic path or consider a brand new strategic path. The process is continuously iterative and should be carried out over the lifetime of the particular strategic path.

Each phase of the Application Toolkit will now be described in process and the worksheets outlined.

PHASE ONE: MAP STRATEGIC PATH

Phase one is made up of five worksheets. Each of the worksheets will now be described in detail. It is important to note that they are relatively simple and are designed for managers to use quickly and easily.

Worksheet 8.1. Outline the Strategic Path: Four Major Strategic Bundles

- With your team, identify, outline, and list in detail the major individual bundles of technologies, product functionalities, market networks, and end-user segments. The list should be of the critical characteristics of each bundle organized by importance. This important analysis may require the inputs of other functional experts to the team and other managers and staff. You are likely to see huge gaps in your strategy.
- For the technologies bundle, the most important and critical technologies that will be the basis for competitive differentiation should be listed in high importance. The objective is not to list all of the technologies that are involved, but the most critical and differentiated ones. These should include not only your technologies, but the adopted and surrounding technologies and supply- and market-side enabling technologies that are critical to your customer solution.
- The bundle of product functionalities should be ordered in terms of importance, the most important being those that are critical to the particular segment of end-user customers and upon which you can establish the highest differentiation. The list of product functionality characteristics should not be an exhaustive list of all of the functionalities but of the most critical to establishing competitive differentiation.
- Market networks should be carefully and thoroughly mapped and the major members identified in terms of their importance to the end user and to delivery of the functionality bundle to end users. Again, the importance measure for market networks is that which produces the greatest differentiation to end users.

WORKSHEET 8.1. Outline the strategic path: Critical strategic choices.

	Technologies	Product functionality	Market networks	End-user segments
High				
Importance				
Low				

- End-user segment characteristics should be identified as clearly as possible, again focusing on those that are most important and the most identifiable.
- When organizing and identifying these critical strategic choices, a great deal of work may be necessary. The project and transformation teams may have to leave and reconvene when members have had time to work and identify these important factors. This worksheet demands a significant amount of work and is a critical basis for the rest of the strategic path analysis.

Worksheet 8.2. Map the Technologies Competitive Space

- This worksheet should be used to map all of the major competitive attributes of the technologies competitive space, including your developed technologies, adopted technologies, and all of the surrounding enabling technologies.
- The worksheet maps the importance of each technology attribute to its technology differentiation. It is critical to identify which of the numerous technologies belong in the high differentiation/high importance to solution area. This is a potential hot zone in this area of the strategic path.

Worksheet 8.3. Map the Product Functionalities Competitive Space

- This worksheet is designed to organize all of the critical functionality attributes of the solution and map them on both the basis of their importance to the solution and how much competitive differentiation you can create.
- Again, the target for this worksheet is to try to find as many high-importance functionality dimensions on which you can also get high differentiation.

Worksheet 8.4. Map the Market Networks Competitive Space

- This worksheet allows you to map market networks and the major members of those networks against the highest potential end-user segments.

WORKSHEET 8.2. Map the technologies competitive space (S1).

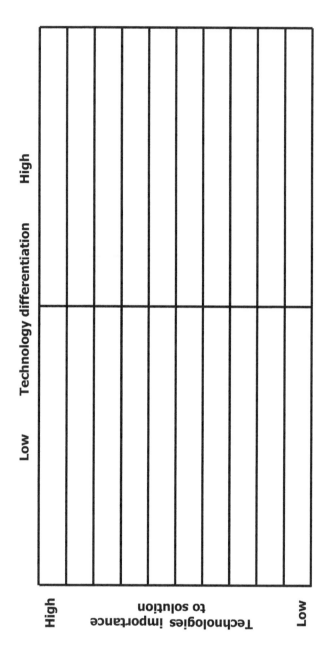

WORKSHEET 8.3. Map the product functionalities competitive space (S2).

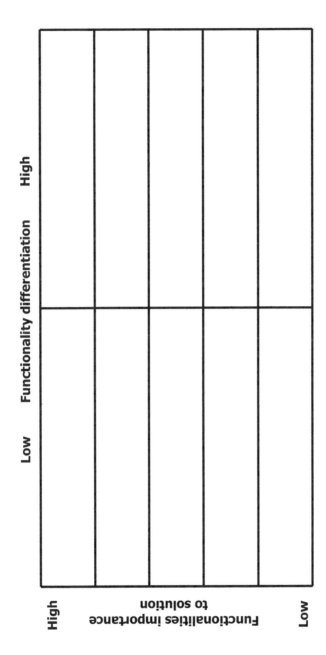

WORKSHEET 8.4. Map the market networks competitive space (S3).

	End-user segments		
High			
Market networks importance			
Low			

Market networks

- The team may have to use other related spreadsheets and out-lines of the market network to identify all the critical members.
- The objective is not to identify all of the market network players and all dimensions of end-user segments but to identify the highest potential segments and the most important members of the market network to reach those end-user segments.

Worksheet 8.5. Map the End-User Segment Competitive Space

- The team should recognize, initially, no more than three or fewer major end-user segments.
- As the worksheet shows, the important task in organizing these segments is identifying them in terms of potential size, defined as their potential for earning high net cash flow.
- Once the segments have been identified, the purpose is to clearly outline as many attributes that define the segment as clearly as possible.

PHASE TWO: IDENTIFY PROBLEMS, CONSTRAINTS, AND INFORMATION NEEDS

At the end of phase one, a clearly defined strategic path should be in place. The purpose of phase two is for the team to identify major forces and barriers they see when going down the strategic path. In addition, the team needs to start keeping an inventory of information needs that market research and other analysis can address. In taking an initial look at a strategic path, it is likely that many uncertainties and many factors will influence the success of the strategic path on which more information is needed. It is important to prioritize these information needs in the order of their significance and importance impact on the net cash flow and success of the particular strategic path.

WORKSHEET 8.5. Map end-user segment competitive space (S4).

End-user segments

Large			
Segment size potential			
Small			

PHASE THREE: MAP THE SIX
TRANSFORMATION PROCESSES

Phase three is one of the most important phases in strategic-path analysis. It assumes that the team has identified a reasonably clear strategic path and choices of technologies, product functionalities, market networks, and end-user segments. Now the task is to identify how the six major transformation processes will be carried out in synergistically integrating and transforming these four major strategic bundles. Worksheets 8.6 through 8.12 allow managers to map the major strategic bundles onto one another to identify hot zones: areas of differentiation, focus, and synergy.

Worksheet 8.6. Mapping the Technology→Product Functionality Transformation Process

- Organize the technologies bundle in order of the most highly differentiated and critical technologies in the solution.
- Similarly, identify and order the product functionalities bundle in the most critical order of attribute differentiation.
- Look for synergies and connections between the technologies bundle and product functionalities bundle that can create hot zones in which you can create and build differentiation in the other and vice versa. You shouldn't expect to find too many of these.

Worksheet 8.7. Mapping the Technology→Market Networks Transformation Process

- Organize the technologies bundle, but this time in order of the differentiation they can produce for the market networks. It is important to look at the characteristics of the technology that will be most critical to the market networks.
- On the market networks side, organize the characteristics of the major members in the market network in terms of their utilization of the product solution. Try to identify the attributes capable of producing the highest differentiation with respect to the technologies bundle that you're looking at.

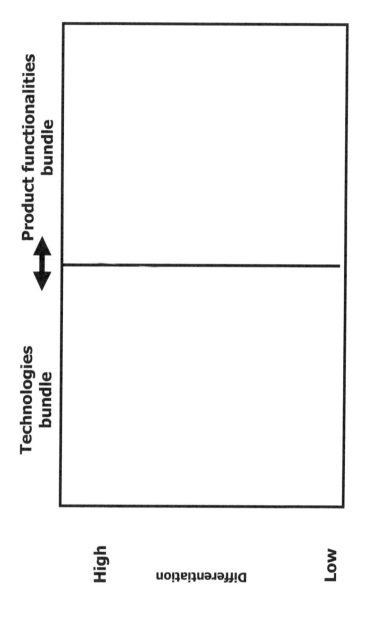

WORKSHEET 8.6. Mapping the technology→product functionality transformation process (T1).

WORKSHEET 8.7. Mapping the technology→market networks transformation process (T2).

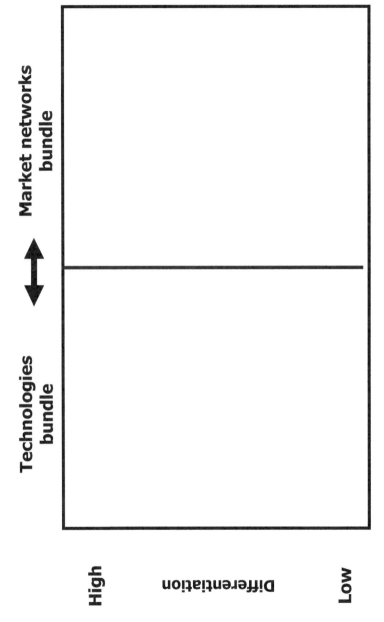

Technologies bundle

Market networks bundle

High

Differentiation

Low

Worksheet 8.8. Mapping the Technology→End-User Segment Transformation Process

- The technologies bundle needs to be organized to recognize the highly differentiated technologies attributes capable of having an impact on end-user segments.
- The end-user segments have to be described and organized on the extent to which they are differentiated.
- The objective here is to look for synergies and hot zones between the technologies bundle and the end-user segment bundles. Also look for problems in terms of end users adapting to the technology.

Worksheet 8.9. Mapping the Product Functionalities→Market Networks Transformation Process

- The product functionalities bundle needs to be organized on the attributes that can create the highest levels of differentiation with respect to the market networks bundle.
- Similarly, the market networks bundle needs to be organized on the critical members and attributes of the market networks that will have the greatest impact on delivering the differentiation in the product functionalities bundle.
- The objective here is to identify highly differentiated product functionalities and market network characteristics that can create synergies, focus, and differentiation between the two: the hot zones.

Worksheet 8.10. Mapping the Product Functionalities→End-User Segment Transformation Process

- Focus on the product functionalities attributes that will have the greatest differentiating characteristics to the end-user segments.
- Focus on the end-user segment attributes that will have the greatest impact on product functionality differentiation.
- Try to identify hot zones, which are product functionality characteristics and end-user segment characteristics that, together, reinforce focus, synergy, and differentiation.

WORKSHEET 8.8. Mapping the technology→end-user segment transformation process (T3).

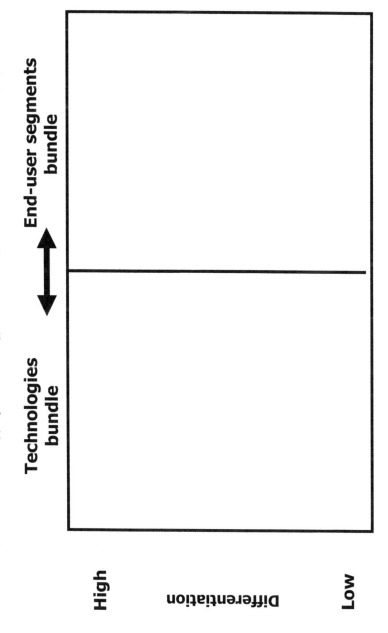

WORKSHEET 8.9. Mapping the product functionalities→market networks transformation process (T4).

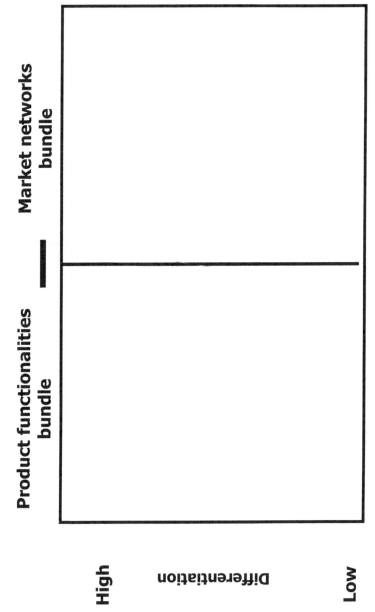

WORKSHEET 8.10. Mapping the product functionalities→end-user segments transformation process (T5).

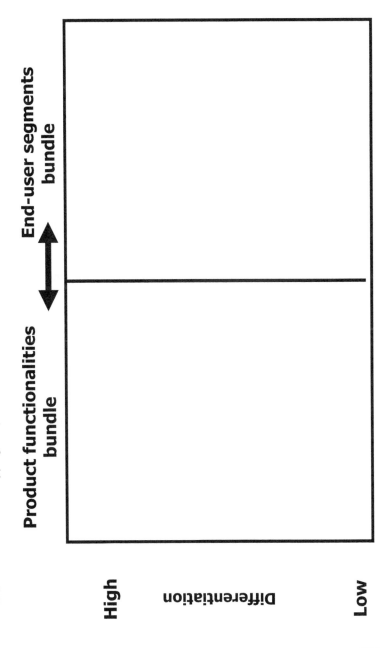

Product functionalities bundle

End-user segments bundle

High

Differentiation

Low

Worksheet 8.11. Mapping the Market Networks→End-User Segments Transformation Process

- Attributes of the market network bundle need to be organized by their differentiation impact on end-user segments.
- Characteristics of end-user segments need to be organized on the characteristics of the segment that will be most affected by the market networks that serve them.
- Try to create and recognize hot zones for end-user attributes and market networks attributes that can create differentiation, focus, and synergy.

Worksheet 8.12. Identify Major Differentiation and Synergies: Hot Zones

Worksheet 8.12 is a summary worksheet for the previous transformation-process worksheets. The critical stages in working with Worksheet 8.12 are as follows:

- The first task is to review the previous worksheets on transformation processes and identify the major areas of positive differentiation that can be created in each one of the six transformation processes.
- The second major task is to take a look at negative differentiation to try to identify problems and challenges that are present in not only each of the decision areas but in the transformation processes that will have to be overcome by strategic change.
- The overall purpose of Worksheet 8.12 is to focus on a few major areas of positive differentiation and to recognize a few major negative differentiation problems that can be pursued and overcome in the strategy. This worksheet really summarizes the previous six.

PHASE FOUR: ESTIMATE CASH FLOWS

The last two worksheets enable managers and teams to make fast and detailed estimates of the net cash flows for the first ten years of the strategic path's implementation. These estimates may be crude or

WORKSHEET 8.11. Mapping the market networks→end-user segments transformation process (T6).

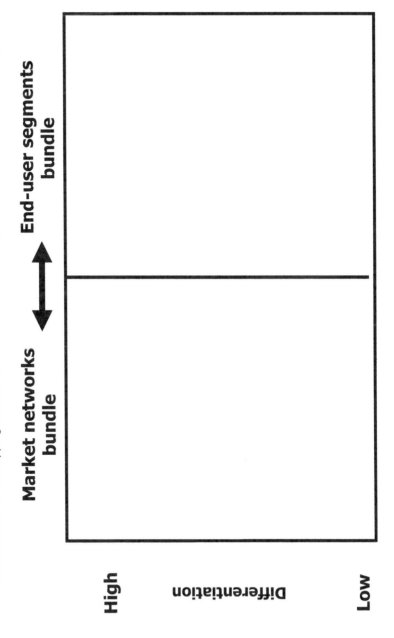

WORKSHEET 8.12. Identifying major differentiation synergies in transformation processes.

	T1	T2	T3	T4	T5	T6
Positive differentiation						
Negative differentiation						

they may be more precise as time progresses. Different elements may have greater or lesser aspects of validity. The objective here is to get, as early as possible, estimates of the cash flow coming out of the strategic path and to identify where the greatest uncertainties are to firm up these estimates. There are two alternative methods for estimating cash flows.

Worksheets 8.13a and 8.13b. Estimate Net Cash Flows (Unit Basis)

These worksheets assume that the product has an identifiable unit so that the cash flows can be estimated in terms of the units of the product sold. The following estimates need to go into the worksheets:

- Estimates of the units sold per year of the product, for as many years as makes sense in the situation.
- Estimates of the unit margin for the product (unit price in dollars minus the unit variable cost in dollars). The unit margin is in dollars per unit.
- Estimates of the positive yearly cash flows from the product (units/year times unit margin), and is in dollars per year.
- Estimates of fixed costs (dollars per year). These fixed cost estimates are negative cash flows, and may require detailed supporting analysis on other worksheets with final sum input to these particular worksheets.
- Investments need to be estimated for the first few years. These investments are in dollars per year negative cash flow required to support the investment in terms of interest and capital repayments, not the amount of the investment itself.
- Estimates of the yearly net cash flows from the product (positive cash flows minus negative cash flows).

It is important to estimate these yearly net cash flows over as long a time horizon as is appropriate in the situation. The worksheets shown here can be supplemented with many other worksheets, but these are useful summary worksheets.

When making these estimates of yearly net cash flows, many concerns will be raised about the validity of the estimates and their sensitivity. These are very important.

WORKSHEET 8.13a. Strategic path cash flow estimator (unit basis).

Cash flow	Year									
	1	2	3	4	5	6	7	8	9	10
Positive										
Unit price	15.00	15.00	15.00	21.00	22.00	22.00	24.00	25.00	26.00	27.00
Unit variable cost	7.00	7.00	7.00	10.00	9.00	9.00	9.00	8.00	8.00	8.00
Unit margin	8.00	8.00	8.00	11.00	13.00	13.00	15.00	17.00	18.00	19.00
Unit sales (000s)	1,000	1,000	1,000	1,000	1,000	1,000	1,000	1,000	1,000	1,000
Positive cash flow (000s)	8,000	8,000	8,000	11,000	13,000	13,000	15,000	17,000	18,000	19,000
Negative (000s)										
Fixed costs	20,000	10,000	10,000	10,000	5,000	5,000	5,000	5,000	5,000	5,000
Investments	30,000	1,000	1,000	20,000	1,000	1,000	1,000	1,000	1,000	1,000
Investments × 20 percent	6,000	200	200	4,000	200	200	200	200	200	200
Negative	26,000	10,200	10,200	14,000	5,200	5,200	5,200	5,200	5,200	5,200
Net	(18,000)	(2,200)	(2,200)	(3,000)	7,800	7,800	9,800	11,800	12,800	13,800
Cumulative	(18,000)	(20,200)	(22,400)	(25,400)	(17,600)	(9,800)	–	11,800	24,600	38,400

Note: Parentheses indicate negative net cash flow.

WORKSHEET 8.13b. Annual cash flows (years 1-10).

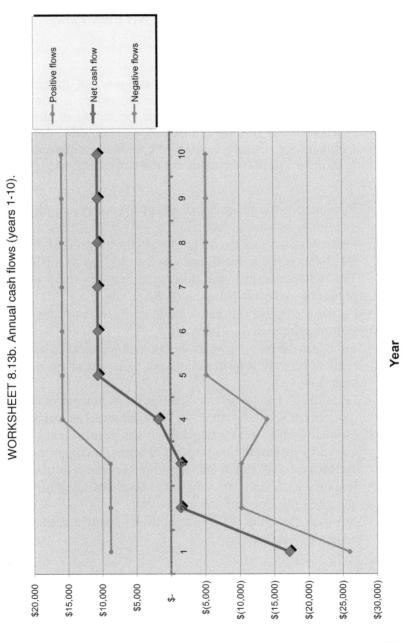

Worksheets 8.14a and 8.14b. Estimate Net Cash Flows (Revenue Basis)

In the case of a particular strategic path, you can use either these worksheets or the previous to estimate the net cash flows. These worksheets are for situations in which the nature of the product makes it difficult to get unit estimates for the product and the cash flow estimates are, therefore, based on revenue estimates. The following estimates need to be made for the worksheet:

- Revenue for the product in each of the few years (dollars per year gross revenue at factory).
- Percentage margin: the dollar margin for the product divided by the dollar revenue for the product, expressed as a percentage. The dollar margin is the difference between the price of the product and the variable cost of the product.
- Positive cash flow estimates, made by the revenue times the percent margin, in dollars per year.
- Similar to the previous worksheets, detailed fixed cost estimates need to be estimated in dollars per year. These are a negative cash flow.
- Investments for the product, estimated as a negative cash flow (dollars per year). Again, as in Worksheets 8.13a and 8.13b, the estimates have to be articulated in the negative cash flow required to sustain the investment in terms of capital repayment and interest costs rather than the amount of the investment itself.
- Negative cash flow: the sum of the fixed costs and investments negative cash flows in dollars per year.
- Net cash flow: the difference between positive cash flow and negative cash flow.

Similar to Worksheets 8.13a and 8.13b, Worksheets 8.14a and 8.14b are summary worksheets of cash flows, and behind these summaries is a lot of detail. The purpose of the worksheets is to summarize them in an easily viewable form so that managers can get a sense of the gross numbers.

WORKSHEET 8.14a. Strategic path cash flow estimator (% margin basis).

Cash flow	Year									
	1	2	3	4	5	6	7	8	9	10
Positive										
Revenue	35,000	35,000	35,000	35,000	35,000	35,000	35,000	35,000	35,000	35,000
Percent margin	25	25	25	45	45	45	45	45	45	45
Positive	8,750	8,750	8,750	15,750	15,750	15,750	15,750	15,750	15,750	15,750
Negative (000s)										
Fixed costs	20,000	10,000	10,000	10,000	5,000	5,000	5,000	5,000	5,000	5,000
Investments	30,000	1,000	1,000	20,000	1,000	1,000	1,000	1,000	1,000	1,000
Investments × 20 percent	6,000	200	200	4,000	200	200	200	200	200	200
Negative	26,000	10,200	10,200	14,000	5,200	5,200	5,200	5,200	5,200	5,200
Net	(17,250)	(1,450)	(1,450)	1,750	10,550	10,550	10,550	10,550	10,550	10,550
Cumulative	(17,250)	(18,700)	(20,150)	(18,400)	(7,850)	2,700	13,250	23,800	34,350	44,900

Note: Parentheses indicate negative net cash flow.

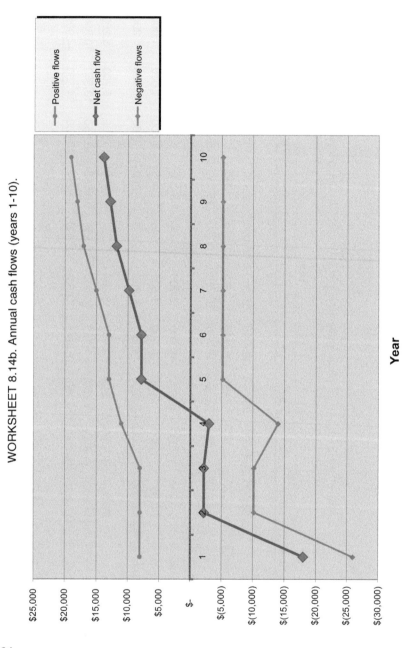

WORKSHEET 8.14b. Annual cash flows (years 1-10).

Year

PHASE FIVE: REVISE AND REMAP
STRATEGIC PATHS

The series of worksheets outlined in this chapter enable and encourage managers and teams to clearly identify a strategic path based on a bundle of technologies, product functionalities, market networks, and end-user segments. The worksheets then enable managers to search for hot zones: connections that produce synergies, focus, and differentiation across the major strategic choices.

Last, the worksheets enable managers to convert these clear strategic paths and the differentiation they produce into evolving and continuous estimates of cash flow. In going through these worksheets, numerous questions, constraints, and problems will arise, and they should be carefully noted. Using the worksheets, and all of the accompanying analyses, needs to be a highly iterative and ongoing process for management teams. Managers frequently find in their first iteration through that much lack of clarity about the strategic path itself occurs and about the synergies and connections within. In phase five, the management team may conclude they should take a look at a significantly revised or new strategic path and go through the process again.

Notes

Chapter 1

1. A.R. Fusfeld, How to put technology into corporate planning, in R.A. Burgelman, M.A. Maidique, and S.C. Wheelwright (eds.), *Strategic management of technology and innovation* (New York: McGraw Hill, 2001), p. 62.

2. P. Kennedy, Report on business, *The Globe and Mail.* Toronto, Canada, July 17, 2004, p. B6.

3. Ibid.

4. Ibid.

5. Ibid.

6. A. Ryans, R. More, D. Barclay, and T. Deutscher, *Winning market leadership: Strategic market planning for technology-driven businesses* (West Sussex, England: John Wiley & Sons Ltd., 2000).

7. G.H. Gaynor, Exploiting product cycle time, *European Management Review,* spring 1993, pp. 3-43.

8. Ibid.

9. E.B. Roberts and M.H. Meyer, Product strategy and corporate success, *European Management Review,* spring 1991, pp. 4-18.

10. Ibid.

11. R.A. Burgelman, M.A. Maidique, and S.C. Wheelwright, *Strategic management of technology and innovation* (New York: McGraw Hill, 2001), p. 36.

12. Ibid.

Chapter 2

1. R.A. Burgelman and L.R. Sayles, *Inside corporate innovation* (New York: Free Press, 1986).

2. R.J. Dolan, Harvard Business School Case, Northern Telecom, ICH 9-593-103, 1993.

3. R.A. Burgelman, M.A. Maidique, and S.C. Wheelwright (eds.), *Strategic management of technology and innovation* (New York: McGraw Hill, 2001), p. 57.

4. E.B. Roberts and M.H. Meyer, Product strategy and corporate success, *European Management Review,* spring 1991, pp. 4-18.

5. J. Gourville, "Biopure Corporation," Harvard Business School Case 9-598-150, revised May 27, 1999.

6. Zenith Minisport Laptop Computer, accessed August 4, 2005, from <http://incolor.inebraska.com>.

7. "Vision, meet reality," *The Economist,* September 2, 2004, pp. 63-65.

8. Ibid.

9. Ibid.
10. Ibid., p. 64.
11. Ibid.
12. R.A. Bettis and M.A. Hitt, The new competitive landscape, *Strategic Management Journal,* 1995; 16: 17-19.
13. Ibid., p. 18.
14. E. von Hippel, *The sources of innovation* (New York: Oxford University Press, 1988).
15. J.L. Bower and C.M. Christensen, Disruptive technologies: Catching the wave, *Harvard Business Review,* January-February 1995, pp. 43-53, p. 43.

Chapter 3

1. C. Wong, "Ballard sells subsidiary to car makers Ford, Daimler," *Toronto Star,* February 5, 2005, p. G14.
2. Ibid.
3. Ibid.
4. Ibid.
5. Ibid.
6. F. Kodoma, Technology fusion and the new R and D, *Harvard Business Review,* July-August 1992, pp. 70-78.
7. N.C. Robertson, Technology acquisition for corporate growth, European Management Review, summer 1992, pp. 36-40.
8. Allied Business Intelligence, Report on portable fuel cell markets, June 6, 2000; available online at <http://www.abiresearch.com/abiprdisplay.jsp?pressid=275>.

Chapter 6

1. S. Ward and Y. Yang, A letter from our chairman and our CEO (press release, December 10, 2004; available online at <www.pc.ibm/us/lenovo/message.html>).
2. J. Gourville, "Biopure Corporation," Harvard Business School Case No. 9-598-150, revised May 27, 1999.

Index

Page numbers followed by the letter "f" indicate figures; those followed by the letter "t" indicate tables.

T - #0101 - 160425 - C260 - 212/152/14 - PB - 9780789030214 - Gloss Lamination